MEYNE WYATT is an award-winning Wongutha-Yamatji writer, director and performer. *City of Gold* is Meyne's debut play. It was shortlisted for the 2020 Victorian Premier's Literary Award and the NSW Premier's Literary Award for Drama. At the 2020 Sydney Theatre Awards, *City of Gold* was nominated for Best New Australian Work and Meyne won Best Male Actor in a Leading Role for his performance in the play. In 2022, Meyne published his first children's book, *Maku*, with Pan Macmillan, which he wrote and illustrated. In 2020, Meyne was awarded the Packing Room Prize in the Archibald Prize for his self-portrait. Meyne is developing *City of Gold* into a TV series with Bunya Productions and is under commission to write a new play for Sydney Theatre Company. Meyne's first short film, which he wrote and will direct, is produced by Bunya Productions and supported by Screen Australia. Meyne wrote a one-hour episode for Netflix's *Heartbreak High* and is writing an episode for season three of *Total Control* for the ABC. After graduating from NIDA as an actor, Meyne's performance in Lachlan Philpott's *Silent Disco* at Griffin Theatre Company earned him the Sydney Theatre Award for Best Newcomer. Meyne's TV credits include *The Broken Shore* and *Redfern Now*, for which he earned nominations for Most Outstanding Newcomer at the 2014 Logie Awards and an AACTA Award for Best Lead Actor in a Television Drama. From 2014 to 2016, Meyne appeared in *Neighbours*, making history as the first Indigenous actor to join the main cast. He has also appeared in *Black Comedy*, *The Leftovers*, *Mystery Road*, *Les Norton* and *Preppers*. For film, Meyne has featured in *The Sapphires*, *The Turning* and *Strangerland*.

CITY OF GOLD

MEYNE WYATT

CURRENCY PRESS
The performing arts publisher

CURRENCY PLAYS

First published in 2019
by Currency Press Pty Ltd,
PO Box 2287, Strawberry Hills, NSW, 2012, Australia
enquiries@currency.com.au
www.currency.com.au

This revised edition first published in 2022.

Typeset by Currency Press.
Cover features Meyne Wyatt for Sydney Theatre Company, 2022.
Photo by Rene Vaile.
Cover design by Katy Wall for Currency Press.

Currency Press acknowledges the Traditional Owners of the Country on which we live and work. We pay our respects to all Aboriginal and Torres Strait Islander Elders, past and present.

NATIONAL LIBRARY OF AUSTRALIA

A catalogue record for this book is available from the National Library of Australia

Contents

Playwright's note

I had the privilege to perform the original production of *City of Gold* in 2019 with Griffin Theatre Company and Queensland Theatre on Gadigal Land and in Meanjin. In 2022, with a whole new production, I performed the play on Gadigal again, this time with Sydney Theatre Company and in Boorloo with Black Swan Theatre Company.

The first time around, I had a chip on my shoulder. Something to prove. I was angry at the world. My dad had passed, I was grieving. I was disillusioned with my industry. Then a relative of mine, a fourteen-year-old-boy, had been killed in my home town, Kalgoorlie. The white man responsible for his death had gotten off. So with this play, I had something to say. Particularly about so-called australia and racism. And I said it, loudly. It got me on ABC's *Q&A*. Performing it has changed my life.

In the time between the first run and the second, the world had changed. Covid was a huge factor in that. But in a lot of ways, the world had not changed. In 2020, the #BlackLivesMatter movement went global after the murder of George Floyd on Turtle Island, which brought a new focus to the Black Deaths in Custody here in this country. Only months after the first production of *City of Gold* in 2019, Aboriginal teen Kumanjayi Walker was shot and killed by a white police officer. In the last week of rehearsals for the second production in 2022, that cop got off.

At the time of writing, there have been 500-plus Aboriginal Deaths in Custody and not one conviction for any of the people responsible for any of those deaths. My play talks about and depicts the injustice of it all. #StopAboriginalDeathsInCustody #BlackLivesMatter

Meyne Wyatt
July 2022

I dedicate this play to my dad, Brian Wyatt

City of Gold was first co-produced by Queensland Theatre Company and Griffin Theatre Company at the Bille Brown Theatre, Brisbane, on 29 June 2019, transferring to the SBW Stables Theatre, Sydney on 26 July 2019, with the following cast:

BREYTHE BLACK	Meyne Wyatt
CARINA BLACK	Shari Sebbens
MATEO BLACK	Mathew Cooper
CLIFFHANGER	Jeremy Ambrum
DAD	Maitland Schnaars
DIRECTOR / SIMMONDS / AC	Christopher Stollery
WHITMAN / ANDREWS / REPORTER	Anthony Standish

Director, Isaac Drandic
Assistant director, Shari Indriani
Set designers, Simone Tesorieri and Simona Cosentini
Lighting designer, Jason Glenwright
Composer / Sound designer, Tony Brumpton
Costume designer, Nathalie Ryner
Dramaturg, Paige Rattray
Fight director, Nigel Poulton
Directorial observation, Hannah Belanszky
Stage manager, Khym Scott
Assistant stage manager, Ella Griffin

CHARACTERS

BREYTHE, late 20s, early 30s

MATEO, mid 30s

CARINA, mid to late 30s

CLIFFHANGER, mid 20s

DAD, 50s

CONSTABLE ANDREWS

SERGEANT SIMMONDS

DIRECTOR

ASSISTANT DIRECTOR

CREW MEMBER

DOP

SOUND

WHITMAN

ACTING COMMANDER (AC)

REPORTERS

BAR PATRON 1

BAR PATRON 2

NOTE

The play takes place across the past and the present.

Scenes in the past: Act One, scenes one, three, five, six, eight, nine, eleven, thirteen and fourteen; Act Two, scenes one, two, four, five, six and eight.

Scenes in the present: Act One, scenes two, four, seven, ten and twelve; Act Two, scenes three and seven.

ACT ONE

SCENE ONE

Bushland. 'Tribal' music. BREYTHE *emerges in loincloth, with canoe and spear. He places the canoe down. Ochres up. Raises his spear and stands on one leg. His phone rings.*

DIRECTOR: [*offstage*] Cut!
BREYTHE: Sorry …

> DIRECTOR *enters.*

DIRECTOR: That's a slab brother—
ASSISTANT DIRECTOR: Please turn off your phones!
BREYTHE: Sorry James—
DIRECTOR: Don't be silly, we'll go again. But good stuff Breathe. Breathe? Breathe. How do you pronounce your name again?
BREYTHE: Breythe.
DIRECTOR: Bathe?
BREYTHE: Breythe.
DIRECTOR: Breythe?
BREYTHE: Yes.
DIRECTOR: Breythe … Does that mean something?
BREYTHE: Hey?
DIRECTOR: In your tribe?
BREYTHE: /Are you—
DIRECTOR: Is it a traditional name?
BREYTHE: Yeah! Yeah in my language, Breythe means 'powerful warrior'.
DIRECTOR: Does it?
BREYTHE: No, no it doesn't …

> DIRECTOR *laughs.*

It's Breythe, like Braith Anasta, the league player.
DIRECTOR: Oh Braith Anasta! Wait, he's not Indigenous is he?
BREYTHE: No.

DIRECTOR: Got bit of a tan though … Who's your mob?

BREYTHE: I'm Wongutha. From WA.

DIRECTOR: North?

BREYTHE: Kalgoorlie.

DIRECTOR: South?

BREYTHE: The in-between …

ASSISTANT DIRECTOR: James …

> ASSISTANT DIRECTOR *points to their watch.* BREYTHE *goes to put his phone back in his loincloth.*

DIRECTOR: Want me to hold that for you?

BREYTHE: Ah … Yes please …

> BREYTHE *hands the phone to* DIRECTOR.

Thank you. Shouldn't go off now. It's on silent. I just need it on. Mentioned to you last night about my ole man … He's in hospital.

DIRECTOR: Remember now. Cancer?

BREYTHE: Remission. He'll be alright. Always is.

DIRECTOR: How you feeling after last night?

BREYTHE: Hung-the-fuck over. Blame you, shoutin shots.

DIRECTOR: Well do we need to head to my trailer and run through some of the new lines?

> DIRECTOR *pinches his nose.*

BREYTHE: I think I'm good … But there have been some new script amendments, haven't there?

DIRECTOR: Little tweak here and there—

ASSISTANT DIRECTOR: James, we gotta catch this sun.

DIRECTOR: Alright! Better get back to it. Can't be runnin' on Blackfulla time … You look great mate. And on camera …

> DIRECTOR *gives a chef's kiss.*

BREYTHE: Really? Standing here with this wig, lap-lap and spear, I kinda feel like a One-Pound Jimmy from the Two-dollar Coin.

DIRECTOR: Yes! You've got that real *Ten Canoes* vibe. Originally, we had this bloke, he was 'community', from NT. Um, what's that place called? You'd know. Out woop-woop somewhere. Had the look, legit. But didn't have the chops. That's why we got you …

DIRECTOR *grabs* BREYTHE*'s arm and examines his skin.*

But maybe we should darken you up. Make-up?!

BREYTHE: What?! No!

DIRECTOR: Why? Blackface! Scratch that! … It's wrong even if you do it, hey?

BREYTHE: All of it is! That's what I'm trying to say. I feel uncomfortable in all of this.

DIRECTOR: Oh brother. I don't want you to feel like that. I want you to feel empowered. You're our hero! Everyone else here is replaceable. I don't want to upset our star … Why don't I head to the tent and talk to production and the client? I'll be right back.

DIRECTOR *exits.* BREYTHE *watches him. Beat.*

DIRECTOR *returns.*

We had a chat. They totally hear you. Why don't we take this? Strike the spear!

CREW *takes the spear.*

But because we're on location, wardrobe have asked if we can keep the costume. Because to get a new one, they'd have to go back to the production office and we're already dealing with time constraints …

BREYTHE: Yeah … Look, it's fine.

DIRECTOR: Yeah?

BREYTHE: Yeah but what about the canoe? I don't get why I have that.

ASSISTANT DIRECTOR: James …

DIRECTOR: We'll put that over here.

DIRECTOR *moves the canoe behind* BREYTHE *making sure it's still in shot of the camera.*

Now Braid— Breythe!

DIRECTOR *pulls out the pocket-sized script.*

What's your character's name?

BREYTHE: Jack—

DIRECTOR: Course! Let's go for a pick-up! Down on the ground.

BREYTHE *crouches on the ground.*

People are going to be talking about this. I'm tellin' ya. You're gonna be a star.

ASSISTANT DIRECTOR: [*offstage*] Alright! Sound!

SOUND: [*offstage*] Speed!

DOP: [*offstage*] Rolling!

ASSISTANT DIRECTOR: [*offstage*] Slate. 'Let's Change the Date Campaign. BBQ TVC' Scene one, shot two! Pick-up.

DOP: [*offstage*] Mark it!

Slap of the clapperboard. DIRECTOR *runs to the monitor offstage.*

DIRECTOR: You got this Jackey Jackey! … Aaaannnnddd— Action!

WHITMAN *enters to 'From little things big things grow' by Paul Kelly and Kev Carmody. He extends his hands to* BREYTHE, *dropping a lamb chop into his hands.* BREYTHE *smiles and holds* WHITMAN's *gaze, until it's awkward.* BREYTHE *looks to the camera for 'cut'.*

DIRECTOR: [*offstage*]: Aaaaaand cut!

BREYTHE: Shit!

BREYTHE *drops the chop.*

DIRECTOR: Print it!

DIRECTOR *emerges.*

Arms, hairs, reaching for the sky. How you feeling?

WHITMAN: A little emotional …

DIRECTOR: Looks fantastic! A hundred frames, slow-mo, hands, meat; *From little things, big things grow—*

BREYTHE: Thought this was meant to be a barbeque?

DIRECTOR *flicks through his slides.*

DIRECTOR: We're going to jump ahead to our barbie set up now. It's time for our surprise!

WHITMAN: Surprise?

BREYTHE: What now?

DIRECTOR: Our cameo. We've only got him for a half an hour, so we have to be quick. What's gonna happen is … Our 'elders', Uncle um …

BREYTHE: Gary—

DIRECTOR: Uncle Gary! And Aunty …

BREYTHE: Ray—

DIRECTOR: Aunty Ray! … They're going to be lining up for their plate of lamb. Then out of nowhere, appears … Kevin Rudd.

WHITMAN: Oh-my-god—

DIRECTOR: K-Rudd will waltz up to the front of the queue and cut in line. But Uncle Gary, who let's say, is lining up for his second helping, sees what ole Kevin is doing. So, he'll hold up his half-eaten lamb bone and point it at him—

WHITMAN: Holy shit—

DIRECTOR: And Ruddy will feel it! Over two hundred and thirty years of injustices. He'll turn around and say 'Sorry' to every elder, as he makes his way to the back of the queue! Tracking shot: 'You were here first.' Bang! Close-up on you. And you'll say 'Here first? Bloody oath.'

WHITMAN: Nice!

DIRECTOR: Pay our respect to our First Peoples. Then we'll have the Lebs and their kebabs, the Indians and their curry, the Chinese and the rest, all here to celebrate this great country of ours. The Aussie way. To have a laugh, a fair go, over a plate of bloody lamb. Let's not dwell on the past. It's Ben-ne-long time. Let's change the date, so we're all proud of it. Because in the end, we're all boat people.

BREYTHE: Yeah, James this's not gonna fly …

DIRECTOR: Why?

BREYTHE: Because you know, the whole out of Africa theory, which is highly regarded and respected in western culture, well it isn't in the Blackfulla community. We come from this land and this land only. Just because you believe it, doesn't mean we do. You boat people. Not us. I know we want to talk about the whole asylum seeker issue! I respect that. And I get it's an ad, we're s'posed to have a laugh, and the lamb is the star of the show but this is really problematic. So, since we're making changes to the script, on the fly, I've got some suggestions of my own. No canoe. I'm already here. And when everyone else arrives, I can say 'you're welcome'. Because I'm not about to throw my people under the bus for some plate of bloody lamb …

DIRECTOR: Okay mate. I understand, but we're running out of time.

BREYTHE: That's not my problem!

DIRECTOR: Then you're the problem! So, let's take a break and come back when you're the solution.

> DIRECTOR *pushes* BREYTHE*'s phone into his chest and exits.*

> *Beat.*

BREYTHE: Twenty missed calls? …

WHITMAN: That was a bit much. He's just trying to do his job.

BREYTHE: So am I! It's all fine and dandy for him to sit there and write this but it's my head in the ad, not his. I'm the one who's going to get slaughtered for it … No Blackfulla is going to wanna do this. He thinks just by having me here, he's done his job and I should be grateful. But he hasn't done the work. This is disrespectful. What was that Kevin Rudd shit?!

WHITMAN: It's an ad, for lamb. It's a joke. It's not that deep. You'd think you'd be happy they want to change the date.

BREYTHE: You'd think you'd be happy we're lookin' for a date change and not revenge!

WHITMAN: We said 'sorry' …

BREYTHE: You don't get it. Because you don't listen.

WHITMAN: What?

BREYTHE: Nothing.

> *Beat.*

> WHITMAN *sees a bird twittering and dancing in the distance and point at it.*

WHITMAN: Aww look at that willie wagtail!

BREYTHE: What?

> BREYTHE *stares at it.*

> *Beat.*

> *His phone rings.* BREYTHE *knows what's on the other end. The ringing increases then comes to a halt.*

Rob.

WHITMAN: Yeah?

BREYTHE: Tell James I quit …

> BREYTHE *exits.*

SCENE TWO

Hospital Waiting Room, ICU. MATEO *is still.* CARINA *is frenetic.*

CARINA: I was right there. I was only gone for a moment. Everything was fine, was fine. I left for a second! I come back, I come back and they, and they, they were all over him! … If he was white, you think this would happen?!

    MATEO *is miles away.*

What the hell am I going to tell Mum?

    Beat.

I'm gonna get them. All of them. They're all going down, man. They're going down!

MATEO: Who was it?

CARINA: I don't know … Their names were something Andrews, something Simmonds …

    They're all going down. I'll make sure of that … Taking you all to court!

MATEO: They'll get off.

CARINA: No, not this time. Not this time. I was there. I saw it. I saw it all.

MATEO: So … You're in Kalgoorlie. They don't get punished. We die and no-one gives a fuck.

CARINA: But I was there Mateo! I have proof! They're all gonna rot!

MATEO: Yeah … Six feet under!

CARINA: The right way! They're going down the right way.

MATEO: What way Carina? Whitefulla way? White law? Since when has that ever helped us?

    CARINA *pulls out her phone and hands it to* MATEO.

CARINA: I have proof, Mateo. I have proof … So we can't do anything stupid. Okay? … Mateo!

    Okay? … We have to stay the course. That's the last thing he said to me. Stay the course … And that's what Dad always said …. So we have to stay the course … Because if we do something stupid, it'll throw it all away!

CARINA *exits.* MATEO *watches the video.*

CLIFFHANGER:[*on video*] Can't breathe.

CARINA: [*on video*] He can't breathe! He's got a condition! ...

SCENE THREE

The roars of a plane. 'We the People ...' by A Tribe Called Quest is blaring. BREYTHE *enters with a duffle bag in hand. A cacophony of gun shots, rocks, glass, fire, police sirens, and indistinct news reports. A riot.* BREYTHE *is now at Kalgoorlie airport. His phone rings.*

BREYTHE: Yeah? I'm at home ... Home, home ... I can't finish the ad. My dad just died.

BREYTHE *hangs up the phone.*

DAD: Breythe ...

BREYTHE *comes to. Trudges off.*

SCENE FOUR

Press conference. ACTING COMMANDER (AC) *and* CARINA *stand behind a podium in a united front.* AC *is midway through answering questions. Lights flash, rapid-fire questions are hurled from reporters as* CARINA *stands behind with a vacant look.*

AC: We understand there is a significant concern in the community over the events of the past twenty-four hours and emotions are running high. And members of the public have every right to protest, but we encourage them to do so peacefully—

REPORTER: What is the extent of the damages?

AC: Thirteen police officers were injured; six police cars were damaged and there are thousands of dollars in damages to public property—

REPORTER: What's the plan forward to ensure the safety of the community?

AC: Local police will be investigating everyone involved. Several people who were throwing rocks and bottles are already in custody. We will be patrolling the streets overnight, working extra shifts, and reinforcements from across the state will be sent to maintain a stronger police presence in Kalgoorlie.

REPORTER: Does the family condemn the riot today?

AC: The family won't be answering any questions at this time and ask the public to respect their privacy—

CARINA: Riot?

Camera flashes. AC *brings the spotlight back to him.*

AC: Now's not the time. Our priority right now / is for community cohesion—

CARINA: Why are we here?!

AC: Miss Black—

CARINA: You had a chance to speak, state *your* facts. I'm speaking … We rallied today, because my goorta is dead. You killed him. That's why we're here. Report that … We were peacefully protesting, but it was you, who once again responded with violence and intimidation.

AC: / I think it's important to—

CARINA: We were defending ourselves from brutality. Police officers were in full riot gear, forcing elders and children back with batons. People were pepper-sprayed and threatened with tasers. So, don't make us out to be the villains. We're fighting for our lives because you're taking them … There's a divide, in this town, this country. And it's time you acknowledge that! You need to stop seeing us as animals and start seeing us as people!

We're dying because of it! … If it was one of your brothers, your fathers, your sons, you'd be angry too! … The violence ends now! … I don't want to see any other families going through what my family is going through right now. So Wongutha, please, wanti ba! … Vigilante acts are not going to bring him back … We have to channel this rage and anger inside us, to get justice! So that's what we're going to do. We demand it! … Now, you'll have to excuse me, because I have another funeral to organise …

CARINA *steps off as camera lights flash and chaotic sounds of the media ring out.*

SCENE FIVE

Mum's house. MATEO *throws darts at the board, pulls them out and repeats.*

> CLIFFHANGER *sits. Beat.*

CLIFFHANGER: Game?

> MATEO *doesn't respond. A taxi arrives.* CARINA *enters from the house.*

MATEO: Look who decided to show up …

CARINA: Shut up.

> BREYTHE *enters, drops his bag.* CARINA *gives him a long hug. They break.* MATEO *hasn't moved.* BREYTHE *goes to hug him but* MATEO *shakes his hand instead. Cold.* MATEO *goes back to the darts.* CLIFFHANGER *walks up to* BREYTHE *and they embrace.*

CLIFFHANGER: Lub your dad … My uncle rest in peace to God.

> *Beat.* BREYTHE *signs 'How are you?'* CLIFFHANGER *replies with a 'sad' sign.* BREYTHE *does too.* BREYTHE *points to Cliffhangar's black eye and signs 'What happened? Did you get into a fight?* CLIFFHANGER *signs 'dickhead'.*

Dickhead.

> *Beat.* BREYTHE *picks up his bag.*

CARINA: Feed in there.

BREYTHE: I toyed with something on the plane … Where's Mum?

CARINA: In the room laying down. Might be asleep but just go in there … Why don't you have a shower first?

BREYTHE: Grog?

> CARINA *nods.*

CARINA: You're campin' in the lounge room. Swag's rolled out for you.

BREYTHE: Thank you … How'd everything go?

> MATEO *throws the darts aggressively at the board.*

CARINA: Talk about it later …

> BREYTHE *heads inside. Beat.* CARINA *stares at* MATEO *until he notices.*

Don't.

MATEO: Not doing anything …

> MATEO *looks at* CLIFFHANGER, *and sarcastically asks.*

What did I do? … Hugged him for fuck sake—

CARINA: Keep your voice down.

MATEO: Not even doing anything.

CARINA: Don't start. I don't want any carrying on … Look at me. Just be … nice.

MATEO: Nice?

CARINA: Yes! Nice! Be nice to him for once in your miserable life.

MATEO: He needs to be set fucking straight. Be lucky if I tolerate him let alone be nice to him—

CARINA: Mum's in the room.

MATEO: If I feel like saying something, I'm gonna say it.

CARINA: After—

MATEO: Say whatever I want—

CARINA: After! It's not your house … He's here now … One less thing to worry about … Got so much shit to do … Got that many people to call … I'll call Mum's side, you call Dad's … Yeah? Yeah?! … Do a Facebook status. Call the funeral director tomorrow— /

MATEO: Carina— /

CARINA: Set the date two weeks in advance, so everyone has enough time to get here— /

MATEO: Carina— /

CARINA: Have to get access to his money. Don't have his bank details. If we can get his super. Been telling him for years to write a will! How we going to pay for this?

MATEO: Carina! Stop! Just stop … Let it marinate in for a second …

> MATEO *pulls out a lighter and cigarette. Lights up.*

CARINA: Seriously?

> MATEO *takes a drag.*

Dad's fresh on the slab and you're smoking?

MATEO: What do you want me to do? Act like you? Run around like a chook with its head cut off?

CARINA: Dad died of cancer! Throat cancer!

MATEO: He didn't even smoke—

CARINA: Get rid of it ... Now!

MATEO: Alright!

MATEO *throws the cigarette away.*

It's gone! I got rid of it! I'm not smoking—

CARINA: Good!

MATEO: Good! ... Fucking hysterical.

CARINA: Boy you better get those words out your mouth right now! I'm not hysterical. I'm acting quite reasonable for the circumstances—

MATEO: So am I—

CARINA: Don't you ever speak to me that way again. I'm the only one here who has their shit together. Only person who's done anything and everything right now—

MATEO: And what? I haven't done anything—

CARINA: You have! Yes. But this is the time we need to stick together—

MATEO: Okay—

CARINA: No!

MATEO: What?

CARINA: Listen—

MATEO: I am listening—

CARINA: No you're not—

MATEO: Yes I am! I'm agreeing with you—

CARINA: Then shut the fuck up ... Shit ... Now I got a goddamn migraine ...

MATEO *walks to the fridge and pulls out a beer.*

MATEO: Go have a lay down. Pour some water on your head ...

CARINA: You want more responsibility? Want to be treated like an adult? Start acting like one.

MATEO: I'm a Lore-man—

CARINA: Big whoop! Want respect? Give some ... This childish behaviour ends now ... Do something for your family. Shit, do something for your dad ...

CARINA *exits. Beat.* MATEO *skols his drink.*

MATEO: Cliffhanger!

CLIFFHANGER: Ay!

> CLIFFHANGER *signs a 'what?'*. MATEO *slaps his hand to go. They exit.* BREYTHE *watches.*

SCENE SIX

Dream: Black Station. 'Lookin' Out My Back Door' by Creedence Clearwater Revival is playing. BREYTHE *is on the back of a ute. Wind in his face, eyes shut, arms stretched out.*

Beat. Two knocks on the roof break BREYTHE *out of the trance. He crouches down.*

BREYTHE: Where?

DAD: Shh!

> DAD *enters behind* BREYTHE.

BREYTHE: Where?

> DAD *points.* BREYTHE *fixates on a point in the distance.*

Goolbit?

DAD: Shh!

> *BANG! Shot of a rifle. Shocks* BREYTHE. *He goes to run.*

Breythe!

> *He stops.* DAD *puts his fist up to gesture 'wait there'.*

Gwarda!

> BREYTHE *is confused.*

BREYTHE: What?

> *Beat.*

DAD: Come here.

> BREYTHE *waits, uncertain what's to come.*

BREYTHE: What's going on Dad? Where are we?

DAD: You have to be a big boy now.

> *Beat.* BREYTHE *realises.* CLIFFHANGER *runs in excitedly.*

CLIFFHANGER: Uncle! Blue-doe!

MATEO: [*offstage*] Cliffhanger!!

> MATEO *enters dragging a full-sized kangaroo by the tail.*

Oi deaf head! You sposed to help me—

DAD: Don't call him that! That's your goorta … Bring it here.

> CLIFFHANGER *picks up the head. The boys place the roo in front of* DAD *and* BREYTHE.

BREYTHE: I thought it was a goolbit.

MATEO: Blue-doe.

DAD: Female Marlu. Female got blue fur, male got red. And them dirty black and grey looking bastards are goolbits.

BREYTHE: Why don't we eat goolbit?

MATEO: Because they taste like shit …

> CLIFFHANGER *laughs.* DAD*'s not impressed.*

I mean, yuck.

DAD: Checked the pouch?

> MATEO *nods.*

MATEO: Wiardu.

DAD: Nothing?

MATEO: Yuwa.

DAD: Pass the wadi.

> MATEO *passes the wadi to* DAD.

BREYTHE: Look at its eyes. It's still breathing.

DAD: Well. Go on.

> DAD *puts the wadi in front of* BREYTHE.

BREYTHE: What?

DAD: Excuse me?

BREYTHE: Pardon?

DAD: Knock it on the head … You shot it … Still alive, see. Bleeding out. Gatda buwa. Put her out of her misery … Come here.

> DAD *brings* BREYTHE *closer and puts the wadi in Breythe's hand.*

This what you have to do. Okay? Nhangatha.

BREYTHE *puts the wadi to the head of the roo. Takes a deep breath. Lifts up for a big swing but* DAD *grabs his arm.*

Wait! No too hard! You wanna hit her firmly.

BREYTHE *lines up again. Taps the roo's head. It wriggles.*

MATEO: Harder!

DAD: Ssh … Bustin yourself.

BREYTHE *is trying not to cry.*

Witu witu …

BREYTHE *hits the roo. It's taking longer than expected. Drawn out gruesomely. Finishes it.*

See. Finished now. This is what you have to do. When you shoot-kill an animal, any animal; it's for food. We not doing this for fun …

BREYTHE: I don't want to eat it.

DAD: What you think Wongi when he lives out bush he gonna go to Woolies or Coles? Go Macca's get a double-quarter marlu with some condongs on the side? No. This is our mayi!

We at the supermarket right now. See this barna, this is your land. You come from right here. Your ancestors lived here. Their spirit is here. In them trees, in this earth and in that marlu. So we take one. Only one. So all the other kangaroos can have more kangaroos … This is your country. Okay? You come from it … We don't come from no God; big Noah and the flood. Whitefullas give you the bible to make you stupid. We not from overseas either; monkeys in the trees. Don't let anyone tell you any different. Not even your teachers at school. History is taught through the eyes of the coloniser. Don't ever forget that. This is your home. Your land. And for that reason, we gotta take it back … Not for gold. Wongi don't care about gold.

BREYTHE: Mum does.

DAD: I know she does. But we taking it back, cause it's sacred. Garnbi … You got that?

BREYTHE/MATEO: Yeah …

CLIFFHANGER *looks at the other boys and mimics their response.*

CLIFFHANGER: Yep … Yep Uncle.

DAD: Gone then grab that googa, bring it to this warta.

>DAD *heads off.* MATEO *grabs the tail and starts to drag it.* CLIFFHANGER *helps.*

MATEO: Dad ... Gwarda. Dad!

DAD: Ay?

>MATEO *puts his hand in the pouch and pulls out a joey with hardly any fur on it.*

CLIFFHANGER: Aww nunefah.

DAD: You said there wasn't anything in there.

BREYTHE: Can we keep it?

DAD: Show me.

>MATEO *holds the joey up to his father.* DAD *examines it.*

BREYTHE: Can we keep it?

>DAD *looks at* MATEO.

DAD: Go on then Mateo.

BREYTHE: Yes!

>MATEO *realises he has to kill it.*

Can I have a hold?

>DAD *grabs the mother by the tail and drags it away.*

DAD: Quick!

>DAD *exits with the roo.*

BREYTHE: Gimme a hold.

MATEO: We're not keeping it.

BREYTHE: Dad just said—

MATEO: Get back.

BREYTHE: Let me have a hold—

MATEO: We can't keep it.

BREYTHE: Dad just said we could—

MATEO: No he didn't. Go over there and play.

>DAD *comes back.*

DAD: No. He needs to see it ...

>MATEO *is hesitating.* DAD *sees that.*

Pass it here.

> MATEO *passes the joey to* DAD.

See that there. No hair. S'not big enough. Can't keep it. Like we did with the mum, we gotta knock it on the head—

BREYTHE: No—

DAD: Have to mate.

BREYTHE: I want to keep it—

DAD: We can't. If it was a little bit bigger, maybe. But it's too small. Won't survive.

BREYTHE: Why?

DAD: Because it needs its mum …

BREYTHE: But I just killed it …

DAD: Shit …

BREYTHE: You just swore—

DAD: I know. I'm sorry. But I have to do it mate. It's not going to be able to live on its own.

BREYTHE: Yes it will—

MATEO: Stop sookin—

DAD: Shut up! Look mate, I'm going to have to do it because it's going to die anyway …

BREYTHE: I'm going to be so cross with you.

DAD: I know mate, I know. But I have to.

> BREYTHE *starts to walk off.*

Breythe! Get back here.

BREYTHE: I'm going to be so upset with you.

DAD: Look.

> DAD *picks up the wadi and smacks the joey in the head twice and throws it away.*

It's dead now …

> *Beat.*

CLIFFHANGER: Nadoo … Sad.

BREYTHE: I hate you … I'm so angry with you.

DAD: Don't worry about it now, it's gone. The ants are eating it.

> BREYTHE *walks off.*

MATEO: Stop running away you sook.

DAD: Stop it … Breythe get back here now! Breythe! I'm gonna count to three. Guthu … Gutharra … Munkurrpba …

> BREYTHE *comes back quick.*

Stand here. All of you.

> *The boys fall in line.*

You want to be a man? This what you have to do. You gotta finish it. All of it. Can't just start something and not finish it. No matter how hard it gets, no matter how much you don't like it, no matter how scared you are. You finish what you start. That's the way it goes. That's life.

> DAD *leads the boys off.* BREYTHE *is left processing. Then follows.*

SCENE SEVEN

Mum's house. CARINA *enters with groceries in one hand, her phone in the other.* CLIFFHANGER *follows behind with more bags.* CARINA *puts her phone on the table, listens to voicemail as she unpacks.* CLIFFHANGER *exits.*

VOICEMAIL: [*voiceover*] 'You have four new messages … Message received at 2:08 … Hi Carina, George Schofield here, from Hutchings Lawyers … I just want to say, I absolutely admire what you said at that press conference, it needed to be said … I suspect you're with your family, so I'm going to be brief … They're moving forward with an internal investigation. I think you'll get a positive outcome because the evidence is there. But if for some reason you don't, and it goes to trial, I want to offer my services right now, *pro bono*, to represent your family in a wrongful death case … Please give me a call, when you can. Thanks. Bye.'

> CLIFFHANGER *returns with flowers.*

CLIFFHANGER: Sissy.

CARINA: They're nice … We'll put them down at the vigil.

> CLIFFHANGER *hands the flowers over to* CARINA.

CLIFFHANGER: No sissy. For you …
CARINA: Oh … Thank you, brother …

CARINA *starts to well up.*

Oh, I forgot. It's your birthday today, inni?

CLIFFHANGER *nods.*

I'm sorry, happy birthday.

CLIFFHANGER *shakes his head.*

CLIFFHANGER: It's okay … I go get the last bag.

CLIFFHANGER *exits. Recorded voicemail of Racist plays:*

VOICEMAIL: [*voiceover*] Carina Black? Do you want to know how many dead boongs it would take to fill all the mineshafts around Kalgoorlie? If you don't keep your mouth shut, you and your other brother will fucking find out …

CARINA *is still.*

'To replay message …'

CARINA *presses 'end'. Beat.* CLIFFHANGER *enters.*

CLIFFHANGER: Sissy?
CARINA: Oh!
CLIFFHANGER: You right?
CARINA: Yeah! Yeah, I'm right …
CLIFFHANGER: Sorry …
CARINA: Na, you right. I'm right …

CARINA *catches her breath.* CLIFFHANGER *goes to exit.*

Clifford!

CLIFFHANGER *stops.*

CARINA: Don't go walking around town by yourself. Specially night time. Okay? Can't trust these mob anymore …

CLIFFHANGER *nods and exits.*

SCENE EIGHT

Mum's house. 'Happy Hour' by Ted Hawkins plays on an iPod. MATEO *enters singing along. He starts playing darts.* CLIFFHANGER *enters singing too.* MATEO *lowers the volume.*

MATEO: It's not a duet. I know you deaf. But I'm not.
CLIFFHANGER: Fuck you prick …

> MATEO *takes a swig from his beer.* CLIFFHANGER *picks up his.*

MATEO: May as well put a tea bag in that beer you been nursing it that long.

> CLIFFHANGER *has a mouthful. It's warm. He puts it down and heads to the fridge.*

Don't go grabbing another until you finish that one.

> CLIFFHANGER *tries to finish it.* MATEO *skols his.* CLIFFHANGER *then follows suit.*

Gorn then.

> *Just as* CLIFFHANGER *opens the fridge,* BREYTHE *enters.*

BREYTHE: Yes please!

> CLIFFHANGER *grabs three beers. Gives one to* MATEO *then* BREYTHE.

Haven't had a bush chook in a while.
MATEO: Surprised you've had one.
BREYTHE: Had a couple on the plane. Can't say they were Export though …
MATEO: Virgin?
BREYTHE: Qantas.
MATEO: Course … What'd you have?
BREYTHE: Hey?
MATEO: What-did-you-have-instead?
BREYTHE: Oh … Lashes …

> MATEO *nods, then looks* BREYTHE *up and down.*

What?

MATEO: Vote 'Yes', did ya?

BREYTHE: What?

MATEO: Dressed like you're going to a poofta's picnic …

BREYTHE: You afraid you weren't invited? …

> MATEO *heads to the dartboard.* BREYTHE *turns to* CLIFFHANGER.

Where you mob been?

CLIFFHANGER: Same place!

BREYTHE: Rodgers Way?

CLIFFHANGER: Mm. Uncle Rick house … Play darts. Have drink. Gone bed …

BREYTHE: Oh okay ...

> CLIFFHANGER *points to Breythe's shoes.*

CLIFFHANGER: Nigh-kee, Airforz one?

> BREYTHE *winks at* CLIFFHANGER.

Err … I'll roll you.

BREYTHE: Go way—

CLIFFHANGER: You have drink, drunk, open hole, tackle you, steal your shoes!

BREYTHE: You wish …

MATEO: Can you even play in 'em?

BREYTHE: Probably not.

CLIFFHANGER: Where from?

BREYTHE: LA.

CLIFFHANGER: Buy me one!

BREYTHE: I'll buy you one from LA-Laverton.

CLIFFHANGER: Pff! Fuckoff. Laverton. Hahaha. No shoes Laverton! Thongs! Dickhead …

MATEO: How much were they?

BREYTHE: Can't remember.

MATEO: Hope you brought your Wet Ones. Red dirt's gonna stick to them like flies to shit.

CLIFFHANGER: Mm. Too white.

MATEO: Be looking like a used tampon by the end of the week.

BREYTHE: Far out. Bit graphic …

> BREYTHE *takes a seat on the stool.*

Haven't heard this in years!

MATEO: What's wrong with it?

BREYTHE: Nothing. It's black.

MATEO: Well what do you want to listen to?

BREYTHE: Na nothing, it's fine.

MATEO: No go on.

BREYTHE: It's fine, really.

MATEO: Well what?

BREYTHE: What?

MATEO: What do you want me to play?

BREYTHE: I don't know …

> MATEO *walks over to the iPod.*

What are you doing? Leave it …

MATEO: No.

> MATEO *stops the music.*

BREYTHE: Okay … Shit. He always like this?

MATEO: You wouldn't know, would you?

> CLIFFHANGER *points at* MATEO *and attempts to whisper to* BREYTHE.

CLIFFHANGER: Grog-Monsta.

MATEO: You're not whispering, munjong.

> CLIFFHANGER *mouths 'Fuck you'.* MATEO *puts on 'Your Man' by Josh Turner.* BREYTHE *chuckles.*

What now? … Spit it out.

BREYTHE: Some things never change.

MATEO: Like what?

BREYTHE: I dunno. Every time I come back here, everyone plays the same old Alan Jackson, Randy Travis—

MATEO: It's not even them.

BREYTHE: Whatever! You know what I mean.

> MATEO *stops the song.*

MATEO: I don't.

BREYTHE: Well it's either one of them blokes or some other hillbilly trailer trash.

MATEO: You don't like country music? What kind of blackfulla are you?

BREYTHE: Excuse me? I was winding you up.

MATEO: You been living in the city too long. Hangin' out with too many whitefullas —

BREYTHE: Get fucked. We never listened to country music growing up. Mum and Dad made sure of that. Where do you think that bumbling bullshit comes from? The racist arse end of the American South. Every song sounds exactly the same. And you're right, for some ridiculous reason, blackfullas everywhere listen to that sing song, lovesick crap when it's the most white-bred, honky-tonk, cracker shit there is! ... So, to answer your question: no, I don't like cunt-try music!

MATEO: What do you want to listen to then, your highness?

BREYTHE: I don't care. Anything. Just making a point—

MATEO: Na fuck that. I don't want to sit here puttin on my music and you criticisin' ...

> CARINA *enters.* BREYTHE *backs down.*

I arxed you a question?

CARINA: *Asked*! Sound like Dad.

MATEO: Take that as a compliment.

CARINA: Wasn't an insult.

MATEO: Well I'm *asking,* what do you want to listen too? And be pacific.

CARINA: Specific.

MATEO: That's what I said.

CARINA: No, you didn't.

MATEO: Pacific!

CARINA: Specific! The word is *specific,* dipshit.

MATEO: Specific, Pacific, Indian, Atlantic, whatever. Who gives a fuck! You know what I mean.

CARINA: Settle down.

MATEO: Fuck off.

CARINA: Mum's in the room there.

MATEO: I know!

CARINA: Calm down. Swearin' around. Who do you think you are, Samuel L. Jackson?

MATEO: Well, what do you feel like listening to?!

CARINA: Mateo.

MATEO: Oh fuck it!

MATEO *pulls the iPod from the cord.*

CARINA: Mateo. Don't come around here drinking and acting up—

MATEO: My Dad just died. I'm allowed to have a beer.

CARINA: Well don't sit here getting pissed all night, swearing and carrying on—

MATEO: I'm not. And you just swore—

CARINA: And don't rock up here tomorrow, half-cut, when we've got shit to do!

MATEO: Go back inside … Do what the fuck I want …

CARINA: You're such a selfish—

MATEO: Piss off—

CARINA: Spoilt brat.

BREYTHE: Alright. Alright—

CARINA: Was my Dad too—

BREYTHE: Don't worry about it, I'll sort it out—

CARINA: / Unbelievable.

BREYTHE: Go inside.

CARINA *exits.*

MATEO: Look at that!

BREYTHE: Look at you.

MATEO: That's every day!

BREYTHE: Turn it down a notch, ay?

MATEO: I turned it off.

BREYTHE: I mean your voice. Lower the level—

MATEO: Look what I have to put up with … That's been the last two weeks. She's not the boss. She don't run everything … Control freak.

BREYTHE: Okay … Well, right now, she's just telling *us* to keep it down.

MATEO: Us? Me. Telling *me*.

BREYTHE: Let's just have a quiet beer then …

Beat. BREYTHE *mouths 'Be fucked'.*

MATEO: How many left?

CLIFFHANGER: Two.

MATEO: You wanna go Star and Garter then, get another case?

BREYTHE: I got no money.

MATEO: Talk shit.

BREYTHE: Murrnda Wiardu!

MATEO: Chuck in for a block.

BREYTHE: I don't have any money.

MATEO: Yes you do.

BREYTHE: No. I don't. I'm broke.

MATEO: We got no grog.

BREYTHE: Maybe that's a sign then.

MATEO: Don't be a fucking tight arse.

BREYTHE: I'm not being a tight arse. I'm telling you I got no money.

MATEO: Aren't you meant to be a big movie star?

BREYTHE: What?

MATEO: Jet-settin' superstar's got no money now …

BREYTHE: Hard to have any when I'm funding everyone else's good time.

MATEO: Still flying Qantas, with your fancy Air Force Ones you got in LA. Drinking your pooncy wannabe craft beers … Big fucking movie star sittin' on set, filming who knows what the fuck, misses the death of his father and for what? You telling me you're broke now?

Where were you Breythe?

BREYTHE: I can't drop everything, every time something goes wrong.

MATEO: You'd think Dad dying would be enough of a reason to come home, wouldn't you?

BREYTHE: I didn't know that was going to be the last time I was going to see him.

MATEO: The writing was on the wall. Shouldn't've left in the first place! I dropped it all to be here.

BREYTHE: You were unemployed.

MATEO: Fuck you. I quit my job!

BREYTHE: Well good for you! My industry's a little different to yours. There's a commitment you make, you can't get out of. I know that's probably difficult for someone like you to comprehend …

MATEO: Walk around here think you're better than everyone.

BREYTHE: Don't have to think Mateo, I know.

CLIFFHANGER: I'm gonna go—

MATEO: World revolves around you—

CLIFFHANGER: Catch ya afta—

MATEO: Had everything handed to you on platter.

CLIFFHANGER: Shit. Where my keys?

BREYTHE: Like fuck. I work hard. And in my business, work don't come around all the time.

    You gotta strike while the irons hot.

    CARINA *renters. Unseen by* BREYTHE *and* MATEO.

MATEO: Dad was heartbroken!

BREYTHE: His heart was broke a long time before he was laying on his deathbed. Where was I? Where were you? Three years, I lived with Dad and where were you? Nowhere! I held him up while he was slowly declining and do you think his recovery was going well, when his own children weren't there. Don't talk to me about feeling bad for not being here …

MATEO: You don't know what it's like to pull the plug on somebody. Put them out of their misery. Because you're gutless—

BREYTHE: Fuck you—

CARINA: Enough!

MATEO: Fuck you—

CARINA: Mateo enough. Breythe—

MATEO: Boy, if I was the old me, I'd knock you clean out.

BREYTHE: Go for it. I'm your younger brother but I'm not little anymore.

MATEO: Sure you want me to bust up your pretty face? Thought that's the money-maker, movie star. Or whatever the fuck you do.

BREYTHE: Step out on the road see what happens.

    They prepare for a fight.

CARINA: You two—

BREYTHE: Been waitin for this moment my whole life.

MATEO: Livin up to your expectations?

CARINA: Stop it—

BREYTHE: Come on then. Let's go, let's go—

CARINA: Cliffhanger!

CLIFFHANGER *stands in between them and holds* MATEO *back.*

MATEO: Work out at the gym a few times you think you're a big shot.

BREYTHE: I'd fucken roast you Mateo! But Mum's always said you shouldn't burn trash.

MATEO: You weren't here to see his face. See him take his last breath. Hear his last words.

You, Breythe. If it was you, laying there, I'd pulled the plug just to charge my phone.

BREYTHE *launches at* MATEO. CARINA *puts herself in the midst of the scuffle.*

CARINA: Oi! Look at you two! What was the last thing Dad said to you Mateo? Stop Drinking! And look at you.

MATEO: Typical … Fuck the pair of you.

MATEO *walks off.*

CLIFFHANGER: Shame. Shouldn't be fighting. You family. Uncle pass away! Sad … Sorry sissy.

I go get him.

CARINA: Let him cool off.

CLIFFHANGER *leaves anyway.*

BREYTHE: What a / fucken—

CARINA: Sit down. What's wrong with you two?

CARINA *looks at the mess.*

Clean this up now.

BREYTHE: When did your last slave die?

CARINA: Just do it … Why do you two do that? Every time. Mateo's drunk. I expect more from you. Dad told him to cut back on drinking and look at the way he responds …

Beat.

He told me to take care of everything … You know in the movies, when the parent talks to the kids for the very last time and it's all beautiful?

BREYTHE *nods.*

Bulldust. It's torture … He said what he said to Mateo, because *he* quit drinking.

BREYTHE: Yeah, I must've seen him touch a beer maybe once or twice. Didn't smoke. And look at that: throat cancer. What are the chances?

CARINA: Wasn't just the cancer. Was negligence. Spent three years at the best goddamn cancer clinic on the other side of the continent, yet it took doctors here less than a week to find a hole in his oesophagus … Three years he practically starved to death. He's only sixty-four.

Was.

BREYTHE: That's young nowadays.

CARINA: For a white person.

BREYTHE: What's the life expectancy of a blackfulla?

CARINA: Sixty-seven, if you're lucky.

BREYTHE: Not helping out with statistics, are you Dad?

CARINA: I could've did better. The day of his diagnosis, I told him to stay over there. I was angry. He wanted to work and keep busy. Thought it would be good for his recovery. But it was killing him. And I know deep down, all he wanted was for me to say 'come back and I'll look after you' … Slept at the hospital every night for the last two weeks, trying to make up for it. So, if anything went wrong, I'd know. So he didn't feel alone. I know he felt alone, for a long time … One morning the nurse came in, Dad thought I was asleep. But I always had one eye open. She had to put that mask on him and he looked up at her like a little boy. Said 'I'm scared'. That machine was too much. So, when the doctor took us aside, and said 'He could live for a week or he could live for a long time, but he can't live without it'. I knew it was time. How much longer do we let him suffer? What's the quality of life? Tried to call you. Left him on a little while longer. But he was struggling. So, we took it off. Made him as comfortable as possible. He waited for you as long as he could … At least you were there all those years taking care of him … I should've looked after him … It's all my fault—

BREYTHE: It's not your fault. It's a bitch.

CARINA: Don't use that word.

BREYTHE: It's … not fair. That's the way it goes sometimes.

CARINA: Won't do that again. Mum's my second chance … I've been crying in the shower.

BREYTHE: It's a convenient place to …

CARINA: When that sad sack of shit comes back, just let him play his country crap.

> BREYTHE *laughs.*

I'm going to bed. You should too … You look like shit.

> CARINA *heads back inside.*

SCENE NINE

Dream: Black Station. 'Bad Moon Rising' by Creedence Clearwater Revival is playing. DAD *with his back to* BREYTHE *skins the kangaroo, disembowelling it as it hangs upside down from a tree.*

DAD: I needed your help, you know?

BREYTHE: I know. I'm sorry. What can I do?

DAD: Too late now.

BREYTHE: I was being an idiot. I'm here now. What do you want me to do?

DAD: Too late now.

BREYTHE: Dad. I'm here.

DAD: Too late.

BREYTHE: Dad.

DAD: Breythe …

BREYTHE: Dad?!

> BREYTHE *puts his hand on* DAD's *shoulder.* DAD *turns. He's white. Terminally ill. Hollow in his eyes. He walks towards* BREYTHE *but slowly deteriorates.*

DAD: Breythe, Breythe …

BREYTHE: Dad … Oh. Dad. Oh. What?

DAD: Where's Breythe?

> *An oxygen tank and an intravenous drip slides to* DAD. *He grabs them to prevent collapse.*

BREYTHE: Dad …

DAD *puts on the mask. It's Darth Vader looking. A hospital bed lands beneath him.*

CARINA *and* MATEO *stand bedside. His breathing gets louder, slower, deeper. Painful.*

Dad I'm here, I'm here …

BREYTHE *can't move.*

DAD: Where's my baby?
BREYTHE: Dad, Dad …

BREYTHE *tries to breakthrough but is held back.*

MATEO: Carina, where is he?

BREYTHE *is so far away.* CARINA *is on the phone.*

CARINA: Breythe you need to get here now!
DAD: Breythe. Breythe. Breythe. Breythe. Breythe.

DAD *starts coughing.*

Breythe.

DAD *coughs more.*

Breythe …

DAD *coughs again. And again. And again. More violently. He starts spitting black blood.*

BREYTHE: I want to go now. I wanna go now. Wake up wake up wake up. WAKE up!!! Dad Dad Dad … No no no no no …
DAD: Aaah … Aaah … Aaah … Aah … Aah … Aah …

BREYTHE *is so far away.*

BREYTHE: I'm here Dad. I'm here. I'm here … Dad.

DAD *disappears. Darkness closes in on* BREYTHE.

SCENE TEN

The street. A drunk MATEO *and a sober* CLIFFHANGER *stand outside a pub. Pulls out a lighter and reaches to* CLIFFHANGER *who give him a smoke.* MATEO *lights it and takes a drag.*

MATEO: Go Ninga Mia road? 'Two-up'?

MATEO *mimics a Two-up throw.* CLIFFHANGER *doesn't answer.*

CLIFFHANGER: Time for bed …

MATEO: Isn't it your birthday? Weak as piss … Give me the keys then if ya gonna be a little bitch … Give me the fucken keys.

CLIFFHANGER *gives him the keys.* MATEO *looks for the car.*

MATEO: Where's the car?

MATEO *looks up the street. Spots it. A paper is on the windscreen.* CLIFFHANGER *grabs it.*

What's that?

CLIFFHANGER: Nothing.

MATEO: What is it?

CLIFFHANGER: Don't worry.

MATEO: The fuck is it?

CLIFFHANGER *shakes his head.*

Show it to me Cliffhanger …

MATEO *pushes* CLIFFHANGER.

Give it to me.

Pushes again.

Give it to me.

And again.

Give it to me!!!

CLIFFHANGER *holds up the flyer.* MATEO *snatches it and grips* CLIFFHANGER.

Don't let people put it over you …

MATEO *lets him go. Reads the flyer.* MATEO *looks up the street, they're everywhere.*

You read this? Read it to me … Go on. It's the least you can do … Read it.

MATEO *puts the flyer in front of* CLIFFHANGER. *He takes it.*

CLIFFHANGER: Cull … a … coo—

MATEO: 'Coon! Cull a coon day. Justice is served. Cleaning the streets. One Abo at a time!'

> MATEO *grabs* CLIFFHANGER.

Why didn't you do anything? Hey? It's your fault … You can't breathe? You're breathing now! So, why aren't you doing anything?!

> CLIFFHANGER *is shaking.*

CLIFFHANGER: Why aren't you?!

MATEO: Maybe I will … If that piece of shit gets off. I'm not gonna lie down and take like you … If I was there, this never would've happened … We all getting this.

> MATEO *gestures 'getting a hiding'.*

After the funeral … Wongi way this is all our fault …

> MATEO *exits.* CLIFFHANGER *starts to cry. Two bar patrons enter and recognise him. They close in.*

> *Blackout.*

SCENE ELEVEN

Mum's house. BREYTHE *comes outside in need of air.* MATEO *is seated.*

MATEO: What are you doing—
BREYTHE: Oh shit! Changing my jocks now, goona'd myself …
DAD: Breythe …

> BREYTHE *looks around for* DAD.

MATEO: What?
BREYTHE: Did you hear that?
MATEO: What?
BREYTHE: Wake up.
MATEO: The fuck you talkin' about? You sleep walkin'?
BREYTHE: What?
MATEO: What?
BREYTHE: What?
MATEO: You high?
BREYTHE: No … I wish.

MATEO: What?

BREYTHE: What?

> MATEO *throws an empty can at* BREYTHE.

Hey!

MATEO: Awake now dickhead?

BREYTHE: Yes!

MATEO: Weirdo …

BREYTHE: You are. Big creep, sittin in the dark like a serial killer …

MATEO: What you jumpy for?

BREYTHE: Na nothin'. Yulda … Forget how freezin' it gets.

MATEO: 'Hot in the day—

BREYTHE: Cold at night' …

MATEO: Grab a jumper …

> BREYTHE, *taken aback by the invitation.*

Those who hesitate, are lost.

> BREYTHE *heads inside. Returns with a jacket and sits down.*

Said that to me after Carina got hit by a car, tryin' to cross the road. You was still swimming then.

BREYTHE: My favourite was 'don't turn your back on the ocean'. Said that after a wave pile drived me onto the ocean floor.

MATEO: You learn the hard way … Do I look guggeri?

> BREYTHE *shakes his head.*

Drank myself sober … Ever do that? Drink to the point you no longer drunk?

BREYTHE: Technically / I don't—

MATEO: I don't want your scientific opinion. Just sayin', feel like I can have a proper yarn, without it being drunken gibberish.

BREYTHE: Yeah I have. Thought I could drive once. Stupid.

MATEO: Drink drive all the time.

BREYTHE: Well you shouldn't. Could kill someone. Yourself included.

MATEO: Country town. Everyone does.

> MATEO *pulls darts from the board, holds them up, asking* BREYTHE *for a game.*

BREYTHE: Don't play games I'm not good at.

MATEO: Never stopped you playin' basketball.

BREYTHE: Better than you.

MATEO: Please child, you're not a pimple on my arsehole.

BREYTHE: Pass me them darts …

> MATEO *hands the darts to* BREYTHE. *They begin a game, taking turn for turn.*

Where's Cliffhanger?

MATEO: Probably Aunty Marlene's.

BREYTHE: She still on Talmalmo?

MATEO: Still in the ghetto …

BREYTHE: Adeline … The council still tryin to call it 'Golden Gates Estate'?

MATEO: Need to demolish that old commissioned housing and build new ones with a proper design. Why is the front door of those houses in the backyard?

BREYTHE: Yeah, ay? You open the door at the front then all of a sudden, you're in the laundry for some reason.

MATEO: Stupid Homes West.

BREYTHE: If it was prime real estate they would. They'd demolish the lot. Should see Redfern these days. Hipster central. High rises built on the Block with ads like 'the Aboriginals are almost gone'.

MATEO: People still sell drugs there?

BREYTHE: Na. Not openly. Not like when we went there, when we were kids.

MATEO: Bikies still peddlin' shit through here …

BREYTHE: Gunja?

MATEO: And the rest … Ice epidemic. Miners demand it, so bikies supply … Got blokes here, earnin more money than they know what to do with. Bored out of their brains. Sexually frustrated from the three weeks they've been laying in their dirty ass dongers, jerkin' it so much, they've got forearms like Popeye the Sailor man. But come knock off, they're smashin' crystal, instead of spinach. When they're in town: FIFO, and can't get a root, they take it out on some poor bastard, some fucken kid who bumps into one of these esky pebble addicts. And because the dickheads watch way too much UFC, they think they're Conor-Fucking-McGregor! Lay the poor fucker out. King hit to coma. Knockin' on heaven's door … Takes an army to bring 'em down. Possessed. Exorcist shit … But most of the brain-dead bastards been smokin' weed since their sweet sixteens, haven't broken out of the dumb-ass phase. And bikies use that. That's why there's a dealer on every street. The green is the gateway drug, straight to the baby blue because it's laced with it. Drop-kicks be switchin' up drugs like they're kids in kindy switchin' up crayons. I want the green one, now I want the blue.

Hardly feel sorry for 'em. The effect is in the name: dope …

BREYTHE: Are you high?

MATEO: You not the only one who can spin a yarn.

BREYTHE: Wipe your chin son, you dribblin' shit. I'm impressed!

MATEO: I love Kalgoorlie, it's home. Wouldn't want to live anywhere else. But sometimes, it can be the biggest hole.

BREYTHE: Literally: The Super Pit … Remember that show *Kalgoorlie Cops*, on Foxtel?

Always enough shit goin' on here for a show like that. You'd watch too, looking for someone you know. Good laugh.

MATEO: Them Wongi's make you shame. Drinkin' and carryin' on. Makes it look bad for the rest of us …

The darts come to a halt.

BREYTHE: Media capitalise on blackfullas. Whitefullas aren't painted with the same brush when they're on the piss, runnin' amok. They be sloppy as fuck Melbourne cup day, killing horses and all. That's double standards.

MATEO: Blackfullas gotta stop doing the wrong thing. They givin' them a reason to call us thievin', junky, drunken, dole bludgers.

BREYTHE: You sounded like a dirty fucken' Lib.

MATEO: I make up my own mind. Not like you blacktivists. 'Black lives matter! Shut down Don Dale! What does sorry mean? You don't do it again!'—

BREYTHE: Shut the fuck up!

MATEO: It's the truth! You don't want your kids locked up? Look after 'em! Can't do that? Shoulda listened to Condomman!

BREYTHE: Fuck me, that Southern Cross tattoo on your arm has taken on a whole new meaning—

MATEO *gives* BREYTHE *the finger.*

MATEO: Sit and rotate. How do these people get in these positions in the first place?

BREYTHE: What, in juvie? Where you get a spit hood strapped to your head and you're beaten by grown ass men? Or put in a home, alienated from your family, your culture. Or in a cell, on the street, left for dead. Those positions?!

MATEO: Which could all be prevented!

BREYTHE: Yes. We need to prevent ourselves from going to jail. We need to stop this second stolen generation. But we're racially profiled, picked on, chewed up and spat out. That's the reason people out there protesting. Gotta make them accountable.

MATEO: With your hashtags and tweets? Just because you shine a light on something, doesn't mean it goes away. You get your likes and shares because people are sheep. Deep down they don't give a fuck.

BREYTHE: Yes they do—

MATEO: No, they don't. Ask your wokies, what happened to 'hashtag stop the forced closure of Aboriginal communities'?! Closed 'em all over WA. Out here; Warburton ranges, Wiluna, Tjuntjunjara. Pushed Wongis off their own homelands, cos they couldn't be fucked maintaining them. 'Living on the land is a lifestyle choice.' Yet, happy to stick a giant drill in the ground, raping and pillaging; on sacred sites! Then bitch about the same Wongis they've made homeless, in town, living like a fringy. Stripped grass off the islands in the middle of the streets, so Wongis can't lay there under the tree, to get cool. Laid AstroTurf down instead. So, when the sun is scorchin'; it melts your skin in that forty degree-plus heat. Turned sprinklers on at night in the parks where Wongis sleep. Kicked them out of their homes then wonder why they're in town … Refugees in your own country. Don't want us here or there. Don't care. Want us dead …

BREYTHE: People care—

MATEO: Not here. Not in the city of gold. Go on any one of these Facebook whinge and whine, crime pages; read the comments. 'Run the oxygen thieves over.' Go to the Exchange Hotel, look at the martini chalked up on the board. Got one-part *gin*, one-part black raspberry liqueur. The cocktail's red and black. You know what it's called? 'The Wounded Boong'. Do you know why they call us that? Because boong's the sound we make when we're hit by a car. And in Kalgoorlie, white people in 4WD's run blackfullas over. Kids even …

BREYTHE: I remember when they used to chase us … I'm glad I live in the city. Racism still there. Hidin' in plain sight. But there they're more inclined to listen to you. You gotta kill 'em with kindness, so they see we aren't just what they make us out to be …

MATEO: Sittin' around holdin' hands, singin kumbaya. You sound like a house nigga.

MATEO *starts to play darts again.*

BREYTHE: Don't use that word!

MATEO: White man been calling us nigga since the day they came here. If I feel like sayin nigga, I'm gonna say nigga. And nigga, you actin' like a house nigga.

BREYTHE: There are good white people, there are bad white people! That goes for anyone, any race. It's annoying when you have to educate and teach them because they're always expected to be comforted and coddled about their ignorance. But the olive branch has to be there, not for us, for ya kids.

MATEO: Breythe, no matter what you do, no matter how many arses you kiss, there's people in this world that just don't like you. That's what I tell my kids. Keep your head down, mouth shut and get on with it. Anyone tries to fuck with you, smash 'em in the face … And if anyone tried to hurt my family, I'd kill the motherfuckers. For that, I'd go to jail … Some of these whitefullas need Wongi punishment … I'm wati. You dithi. That's your problem. You not a man. You lost. And that's why our people do stupid shit. They don't know who they are. They don't know lore, culture or respect. Haven't been put through. Their spirit is lost. Just like you …

BREYTHE: Put me through then …

MATEO: You won't—

BREYTHE: Do it!

MATEO: Gotta make some sacrifices … And I'm not just talkin' about snippin' the turtleneck off the tip of your dick. Your lifestyle. This acting business. To be initiated, you have to be committed. To the land. To lore. To your people ... Can't walk away like you did with Dad ...

BREYTHE: I didn't want to go. Dad told me to. That's why I left. I thought I was doing right by him. Now, I can't get him out of my head. Can't sleep. Can't dream. He's ...

MATEO: Visiting you? That means he's trying to say something to you ...

BREYTHE: It's guilt. Everything that's been festering in the pit of my stomach, coming up to the surface.

MATEO: You either bury it or live with it ...

BREYTHE: That sounds real fucken healthy ...

MATEO: Well, there's people you can talk to now. But not me. Because I'd tell you to take a viagra and harden the fuck up.

BREYTHE: Harden up, grow a pair, eat a cement pill ... You know, supressing your emotions don't make you man ... I'll be saying that to my nephews too.

BREYTHE *moves to head back inside.*

MATEO: Where are you goin'—

BREYTHE: To bed ...

BREYTHE *exits.*

MATEO: Say hello to Dad for me.

SCENE TWELVE

Mum's house. A beaten CLIFFHANGER *stumbles in and drops. He starts to fit. Lights come on.*

CARINA: Who's that?!

CARINA *enters and sees* CLIFFHANGER.

Clifford! Clifford! ...

She rushes to him.

Roll over. Roll over.

CARINA *rolls* CLIFFHANGER *to his side.*

Take it easy. Take it easy ... Just breathe. Breathe ... Mateo!

CLIFFHANGER *starts to come to.*

CLIFFHANGER: No sissy. No. Don't tell him. Pleaz … Pleaz. My fault. My punishment.

CARINA: No, No. It's not your fault. It's not fault … Ssh, ssh. Look at me.

MATEO *enters.*

What happened? You left him out on his own?

MATEO *looks at the state* CLIFFHANGER *is in.*

You can't do that Mateo. These bastards won't quit! They'll kill us all!

CARINA *and* MATEO *help* CLIFFHANGER *to his feet.*

CLIFFHANGER: Sorry brother. I'm sorry. Sorry …

MATEO: Don't worry about it …

CARINA: Help me get him inside, help me get him inside, before he has another fit!

CARINA *leads him inside.* MATEO *waits. He begins to fume.*

Blackout.

SCENE THIRTEEN

Dream: Dad's house. Early morning. 'Fortunate Son' by Creedence Clearwater Revival is playing. BREYTHE *stands.* DAD *enters.*

DAD: Holy Toledo boy! Place looks like a pig sty.

BREYTHE *is discombobulated.*

BREYTHE: I'll clean up after—

DAD: Come on, looks like a bomb hit it!

BREYTHE: I'm gonnu—

DAD: Codswallop! Do it now!

BREYTHE: Alright! I said I'm going to do it! I'll do it! Far out! Not a little kid!

DAD: Can you head up to the shop for me? Get me a chocolate éclair.

BREYTHE: I don't even know what that is …

DAD: Doctor said I need to put on weight.

BREYTHE: That doesn't sound like something you should be eating.

DAD: I'm hungry …
BREYTHE: Do you want to go out and get a feed?
DAD: Not tonight mate.

> DAD *coughs, loud and abruptly. It embarrasses* BREYTHE. DAD *coughs again.*

BREYTHE: You right?
DAD: I think there's a prawn shell stuck in my throat.

> BREYTHE *start to laugh. Pulls out his phone and laughs into it.*

BREYTHE: The bloke thinks he has a prawn shell stuck his throat …
DAD: It's not a prawn shell!
BREYTHE: Hahaha—
DAD: It's not funny …
BREYTHE: Haha—
DAD: It's cancer …

> BREYTHE *stops. Beat.*

Your brother and sister want me to come home.
BREYTHE: What do you want to do?
DAD: If I stop working, how am I going to pay off the house? I can't.
BREYTHE: If you want my opinion—
DAD: I do …
BREYTHE: Do what you want to do, it's your life … Fuck.
DAD: Stop swearing you dilbry …
BREYTHE: This is what I miss, that, annoying, cheeky dag. I thought you were going to get better …
DAD: They said they have to stick a peg in my stomach. This bag is what's feeding me from now on. What kind of life is that?
BREYTHE: It's the only one keeping you alive, mate …

> DAD *puts on the oxygen mask.*

DAD: How do I look?
BREYTHE: Look like Darth Vader … Dad I'm scared.
DAD: No-one's more scared than me mate.
BREYTHE: Do you want me to stay?

> *He nods. Beat.* DAD *shakes his head.*

DAD: Stay the course … Keep doing what you're doing … In this life, no-one's gonna give it to you, you gotta take it … Breythe …

BREYTHE: Yeah?

> DAD *goes to leave.*

DAD: Go … You have to go. This place is not meant for you …

> DAD *'s gone.*

SCENE FOURTEEN

Mum's house. BREYTHE *is looking into the distance. His phone rings. He answers.*

BREYTHE: Hello … I can't … Because the ad is messed up … How much more? … It doesn't matter. I have to be with my family. I gotta go.

> *He hangs up. Beat.* MATEO *is seated.* CARINA *enters through the back door.*

CARINA: How much money do you have?

MATEO: Coupla notes.

CARINA: In your account?

MATEO: Nothing. Think one of 'em has a debit.

CARINA: Fuck … You? … Breythe?

> BREYTHE *shakes his head and flicks a 'nothing' gesture.*

I don't know how we're going to pay for the funeral.

BREYTHE: What do you mean?

CARINA: They won't clear the money. And I don't have all the passwords to his accounts …

MATEO: Isn't it something like wongimagic58?

CARINA: It was …

MATEO: Have you tried it in uppercase—

CARINA: Yes.

MATEO: Capital W? Capital M?

CARINA: Yes.

MATEO: Did you make sure the caps lock wasn't on—

CARINA: For fuck sake, yes.

MATEO: What are we going to do?

CARINA: I don't fucking know.

BREYTHE: Didn't he sign all of the papers?

CARINA: Didn't have the strength to. When he tried it looked like scribble … Bank said it takes weeks, months to clear, apparently. I haven't received child support in that long …

How do you have no money?

MATEO: I got kids too.

CARINA: There's two of you.

MATEO: Got bills to pay.

CARINA: How do you have a debit and still afford to go ragin'?

MATEO: Don't start.

CARINA: You come around here ask me and Mum for money all the time. Does it ever come back?

MATEO: I was going to pay / you back.

CARINA: That's not the point …

MATEO: We'll think of something—

CARINA: 'We'll think of something'! Oh thank you. The great mind of Mateo is going to think of something, yay!

MATEO: Well how are we going to get the money?

CARINA: That's the million-dollar question isn't it? I'll lock in A: I DON'T FUCKING KNOW!

MATEO: Ask them mob.

CARINA: I'm not asking anyone for a goddamn thing, the way I've been treated.

MATEO: You haven't exactly been the most hospitable person in the world.

CARINA: I don't have to be. I have no obligation to make anyone feel better. Dad needed to recover! I don't care what anyone else wants. It's not about them. Everyone had their chance to see Dad when he was alive. Had nothing to do with his health and wellbeing.

That's why I said no more visitors. Don't like me for it, that's nothing new. We're his kids, we pull rank. I'm not asking anybody for a goddamn cent. And if my connection to them gets buried with Dad, so be it.

MATEO: At this rate, we're not going to be burying him at all.

CARINA: I don't grovel Mateo.

MATEO: You're so stubborn.

CARINA *acts like a mule.*

CARINA: Ee-oh, ee-oh, ee-oh!

MATEO: Yeah! That's right, you are jackass!!

CARINA *continues.*

BREYTHE: When I first started working, Dad let me crash on the couch, until I found my feet.

Once I had a bit of cash under my belt, I'd move out. But I didn't. I stayed. Part of me wanted to keep an eye on him. The other, wanted to make as much money as I could.

CARINA: Breythe, what are you talking about?

BREYTHE: All I had to do, was take care of the stores and tidy up. Struggle for him to get outta bed, let alone the house. Bloke was a bag of bones.

MATEO: Ay!

BREYTHE: Looked like a one of them kids from a 'One dollar a day' ad, nadoo … One night, I knock off work. It's the end of the week, home game at Etihad. Come home, jump in the shower, get ready. Twenty-minute walk to the ground, if I leave now I'll make it right on time. He hadn't had a proper feed all day. Fuck all in the house except for some oats and milk. Ask him to make some porridge. He already had two bowls! But I want to make bounce down. Tell him I'll get a takeaway on the way back. He obliged. Let me go. Whilst he sat there hungry as a muthafucka.

MATEO: Oi!

CARINA: Breythe—

BREYTHE: I was arrogant, selfish, in denial. So, I go. Knock back a couple. Couple become many. Get pissed as parrot. Games go for two and half hours, three? Took my sweet arse time. Shit, even went to the pub after. Come home, waltz through the door, no food, smelling like a pirate! And he looks at me … I'll never forget that look. Can't. Won't. Don't …

His eyes. I'm fucking around with life here. Literal life or death situation, for the state he was in. He's barely standing up. So am I. He's livid. Disappointed. Not just cos I let him down, but because I went and got drunk … He was hungry all day, waiting, while I was at work. And there I was making him wait all night. No doubt in my mind I took years off his life in that instance. Later that night, he's coughing his guts up, in the room. Worst I'd ever seen at this point. Tell him to get up, we're going to the hospital. All the while he's apologising to me. I don't want to make a fuss. As if he done me wrong. He's in that position because I put him there. I'm the cause of his suffering. Two, three months later, he's here, on his deathbed.

Fear's replaced that look of disappointment. Looks at me and says, you're the apple of my eye. He's proud. I'm not. This fruit is rotten. I don't regret not being here when he died. I regret not treating him better when he was alive. I don't want be a disappointment anymore. I can pay for the funeral ... But I have to do something first ...

BREYTHE *exits* ... CARINA *and* MATEO *watch on.*

Blackout.

ACT TWO

SCENE ONE

The advertisement. BREYTHE *enters, acting out the advertisement. This time it's a nightmare. Breythe's skin is darker. More stereotypical. Cartoonish. Smile on his face and two slabs of lamb meat in his hands with blood dripping on the floor. He dances with chains around his hands and feet.*

WHITMAN *enters dressed like a white Jesus, cross in his hand.* BREYTHE *is still, in a pool of light with darkness around him. Everything moves past him. Violence, slavery, white-washing. Iconic Indigenous moments play out.* BREYTHE *dances. Then silence.* BREYTHE *is whipped. He's at the bottom of a mineshaft. Everything comes crashing down. He drowns.*

SCENE TWO

Dad's old house. BREYTHE *enters the backyard. Drops his duffle bag.*

BREYTHE: First and foremost, I want to pay my respects to the traditional owners of the land: me. Hahaha! Na na sorry. Welcome. Welcome. Welcome … To Galgula. Kalkula. 'It's actually pronounced, Kalgoorlie!' … Ghost town. Eh, Dad? Was pumpin' in the nineties. Mining boom! Shaka-laka! Fly in-fly out came and killed it. Population: tumble weeds and crickets.

> BREYTHE *whistles a cricket sound.*

'Don't whistle at night' … Well, where are ya Dad?! … Remember we'd play kick to kick, here?

Father and son time. Never told ya; didn't want to hurt your feelings. But really, I just wanted to play by myself …

> *Lights of the MCG light up* BREYTHE.

'He breaks out on the half forward flank, no-one's there, sells the dummy, snaps on his right boot, goooaaaalll!!! The crowd erupts.'

'Yeaahh!!!' … 'Breythe Black, outstanding performance. How do you think you went out there tonight?' Yeah nah, nah yeah, yeah nah, the boys just went out there gave it a four-quarter effort, we know they're a good side, but we were just the better team on the night. 'Thank you. Back to the boys at the desk' …

The MCG lights are gone.

Was never really good at footy. Was good at pretending I was good at footy … One time, you asked if my white friends were racist. 'Do your team mates call you choc? Or cookie? Or coco pops? Have white friends, but remember, deep down, they're always white' … 'Hey Breythe, what do you think he's gonna do with his money?' Who? 'That dude busking.' What do *you* think he's gonna do with his money? Because he's black, you think he's gonna go drinking? I'm always going to be your *black* friend, aren't I? That's all anyone ever sees … I'm never just an actor. I'm always an Indigenous actor. I don't mind reppin'. But I don't hear Joe Blogs over here being called white Anglo-Saxon actor blah-di-blah. I'm always in the black show, the black play. Always the angry one. The tracker, the drinker, the thief … 'You're so lucky to be working.' Suck a dick. It's a job like any other. I don't feel bad for getting pissed off about it. Not one bit. Not one iota. I just want to be seen for my talent, not my skin colour. Not my race. I hate being a token, a box to tick, part of some fucking diversity angle.

Never just a character. And when you are, you're the bastard in King Lear. 'It's because you're Aboriginal.' 'What are you whinging for? Everything's been handed to you. You've never had to work a day in your life.' Aboriginal, Aborigine, Aboriginous. Indidge, Indigene, Indigenous. Indigereedo, Indigireedont, Digereedont … 'Can't you play?' The trees for a didgeridoo don't exist down south, that's why I don't play you fucking twat! 'You're not a real one then. What percentage? You're only part.' What part then? My foot? My arm? My leg? You're either black or you're not! 'Need proof of Aboriginality' Honk, honk, honk!

Wanna do a DNA test? Come suck my blood! … 'How are we to move forward if we dwell on the past?' That's your privilege. You get to ask that question. Ours is: we can dance and we're good at sport. You go to weddings, we go to funerals. No, you're not your ancestors, it's not your fault you have white skin. But you do benefit from it. You can be okay. I have to be exceptional. I fuck up, I'm done. No path back for me. No road to redemption. Being Black and successful comes at a cost. You take a hit, whether you like it or not. Because you want your Blacks quiet and humble … You can't stand up, you have to sit down. Ask the brother-boy Adam Goodes. Two-time Brownlow medallist, double premiership player, captain of the club, hall of famer. Heads down, bums up, shut the fuck up, Goodsey.

Squeaky clean muthafucka. Ask him, he knows … Kid says some racist shit. Not ignorant! Racist! Calling a blackfulla an ape. C'mon man, we was flora and fauna before 1967, actually, correction, we didn't even exist at all. That's only fifty-odd years ago. But he didn't lose his cool. He got it. It was a kid. This was a learning moment. He taught the kid a lesson. Went all Martin Luther King on the shit. 'Australian of the year'! Whatever the fuck that is. But they didn't like that. A black man standing up for himself? Na. You shut the fuck up boy. You stay in your lane! Anytime you touch the ball we gonna boo your ass! So, he went Malcolm X on them muthafuckas! Showed 'em a scary black! Ooh-ga-da booh-ga-da black, throwing imaginary spears and shit. Oh, and did they like that? Oh no, no, no, no, they didn't like that! Every arena, every stadium they booed him. 'It's the way the flog plays football!' Bull-fucken-shit! No-one booed him the way they booed him until he stood up and said something about race. Second he stood up, every muthafucka came out of the woodwork to give him shit. And he's supposed to sit there and take it? Well I tell you right now. Adam Goodes has taken it. His whole life he's taken it … I've taken it. No matter what. No matter how big, how small, I'll get some racist shit, on a weekly basis and I'll take it … Used to be that in your face, boong, black cunt shit. Gonna chase you down the ditch with my baseball bat, skinhead shit; when I was fourteen years old. And that's the shit I actually prefer. At least then I know where muthafuckas stand. Give me that 1960s, KKK, Alabama-like shit. That shit I grew up with. Right here in Kalgoorlie! That shit, I have first-hand experience of. But nah we've come forward. We progressive muthafuckas. We gonna give you that small, subtle shit. The shit that's always been there, but it's not that 'obvious', 'in your face' shit, no, it's that 'Now we can't be seen to be racist' kinda shit. Security guard following me around the store, asking to search my bag. That walking up to the counter first and being served second or third or last kinda shit. Hailing a cab and watching it slow down, to look at my face and drive off. More than once. More than twice. More than once, twice on any one occasion. That shit. Yeah, I'll get that; weekly. Sometimes I'll get it days in a row if I'm really lucky.

That's the kinda shit I'm letting them think they're getting away with. Not for them. For me. Because to be honest, I can't be fucked. Can't be fucked teaching their ignorant asses on a daily basis. I don't have the energy or the enthusiasm. It's fucking exhausting. And I like living my life ... But then. On an occasion. You've caught me on a bad day. Where I don't feel like taking it. I'll give you that angry black muthafucka you've been asking for and I'll tear you a new arsehole. Not because of that one moment. Because of my whole life ... At least Adam danced. And they still pissed and moaned. But it's not just about that one time. It's about all those times ... And you can be black and successful. But they want you to be their kind of black. That tall, handsome, non-threatening black man. Dwayne Johnson! If ya smell what The Rock is cookin'? Why do you think The Rock is the highest paid, highest grossing movie star in world? Because he's in your face and political? Uh-ah ... Because he's a big bald, goofy, fun-lovin' muthafucka! All charming and charismatic and shit. He lifts his eyebrow and jiggles his tits and people pay to see him. Time and time again. But he also shuts the fuck up. Toes the line. Quiet about his politics. The Rock, he sees the game and he's a master at playing it. That's why he's successful ... Woulda said the same thing about Will Smith before he started smackin muthafuckas! Before that you weren't scared of Will Smith! He was the Fresh Prince of Bel Air. He was the dude you could take home to ya mother. He rapped. But he rapped that PG-thirteen shit. And that was cool enough for white people. They ate that shit up. But the second he slapped the other Rock, they spat that shit out ... Keep your mouth shut. Open it; watch em turn ... We'll keep our mouths shut. If you just keep payin' us that money.

We just want that money. We wanna do what we wanna do and look good doin' it. Sittin' up with our fly kicks, chillin'. Feed that family. We simple people. We don't care. We cool with being hood rich … But don't you worry you get it from the other side too. Your own community. I see you. I hear you. I feel you. I gave you the black nod. What? You think I'm a coconut? Say that shit to my face. You don't know me. You don't know where I'm from. I don't have to be a flag beater. You believe what you want to believe about me, I'm only giving you what I want you to see. I don't have to protest my identity. If I want to be put through I can. If I want to speak my language I can. Ngayu Breythe Black, garlu-yurrna … I don't run down other blackfullas publicly. What message does that send? Already got so many people holding us back. You just giving ammunition to our enemies. That's not liftin us up, that's bringin us down … I'm gone give em that Black militant, but when I get there. I'm not there yet! Let me get there … And sometimes, unfortunately, you gotta swallow your pride. Compromisin'. Not that sell-out shit. Sometimes you gotta pull out them knee pads and suck some dick. So I'll play the game. Not cos I want to, because I have to. I don't have the luxury. Chips are already stacked against me. And that's why there's one on my shoulder. So I do it. I'll play. And I'll beat the white man at his game. Black, white or any other muthafucka. Put 'em in false sense of security and then fuck their ass up. But I'll be what I wanna be. I don't wanna be what you want me to be. Never trade authenticity for approval. Be crazy. Take a risk. Be different. Offend some motherfuckers. Nothing worse than being mediocre. Unambitious. I don't want to be quiet. I don't want to be humble. I don't want to sit down … But I'm finding it real hard to stand up … Where are you Dad? I want to wake up and for this all to be a dream. You're dead and it's not a dream …

> BREYTHE *fall to the floor. Pulls out his phone puts it on loud speaker and dials Dad's number. Message bank.*

DAD: [*voiceover*] Ah … hello you've phoned Byron, I'm not available at the moment, but if you leave your number, I'll get back to you when I have the time.

BREYTHE *dials again. Straight to message bank.* BREYTHE *repeats this. The sound slowly fades.*

SCENE THREE

Mum's house. MATEO *sits in the dark.* CARINA *springs from the house, on the phone, mid-conversation.*

CARINA: Yes George. I'm here ... What? ... An indefinite suspension? ...

> CARINA *puts the phone down for a second, panic crying in shock. Then brings it back up.*

I'm here, I'm here. I'm sorry. It's just ... That's fucking disgrace! ... I can understand it, somehow, for Simmonds. But Andrews? That's not even a slap on the wrist! ... Of course, I do!

> *Beat.* CARINA*'s face completely changes at what she's hearing.*

What? ... Who?! When was this?! ... Right now?!

> CARINA *looks up into the distance and sees the fire.*

Oh my god ... I can see it ... Yeah I can see the smoke ... He lives so close ...

> CARINA *is overwhelmed.*

I've gotta go, I gotta go.

> *She hangs up. Looks at the fire. Then screams. And begins to bawl her eyes out.*

MATEO: Who was that?

CARINA: Jesus Christ, Mateo!

MATEO: Who was that on the phone?

CARINA: The lawyer, George ... Did you see that? That's his house. That's Andrews' house.
> Someone set it on fire!

MATEO: What'd he say?

CARINA: This isn't good for our case. First the protest, now this. This is only gonna make it harder and harder.

MATEO: What did he say about hearing?

CARINA: We can push for a wrongful death case ... Says that's the best way forward. Because of the evidence.

MATEO: What's an indefinite suspension then?

CARINA: It's temporary …

MATEO: Sounds like a holiday to me.

CARINA: It's temporary. We just have to move forward.

MATEO: 'Move forward' … You know when Dad was around the same age, six cops dragged him out in the middle of Burt street and they beat him to an inch of his life.

CARINA: I know the story—

MATEO: And one of them cops became commissioner of police. I told you Carina.

CARINA: It's not over!

> CARINA *looks at* MATEO. *He's dirty.*

Where've you been?

MATEO: Bush. Took the kids for a ride to Kookynie. Showed 'em that monument at Mount Catherine.

> CARINA *can smell petrol on his clothes.*

CARINA: You stink …

MATEO: Said see that, Wongis made that …

CARINA: Like petrol …

MATEO: Because Wongis were massacred in that gully in the 1800s …

CARINA: What've you done Mateo?

MATEO: Three white blokes with guns surrounded them. Like you do when we go hunting for malle-hen. And picked them off one by one.

CARINA: What have you done?

MATEO: And even after they admitted to doing it. They all got off, scot-free.

> *Beat.*

CARINA: It's not over. We want the same thing Mateo. I'm wild. I'm batha! But he'll go free if you do shit like this! This isn't justice.

MATEO: That's a message.

CARINA: You have to trust me.

MATEO: I did. I did trust you Carina. But I don't trust them …

> MATEO *exits.* CARINA *doesn't know what to do.*

SCENE FOUR

Mum's house. Morning. BREYTHE *staggers in singing 'The Unicorn' by the Irish Rovers. Stops. Sways.* CARINA *emerges from the house.*

CARINA: Did you just get in? Where's your bags?

BREYTHE: Noodba … Na … Been here a coupla days.

CARINA: What?

BREYTHE: Where is my bags?

CARINA: Where have you been?

BREYTHE: I been … Meekatharra, jail, hospital, jail / Meekatharra, hospital, jail.

CARINA: Mateo. Mateo!

BREYTHE: Nah, fuck Kevin Bloody Wilson. Racist cunt! He's from Kalgoorlie eh?

MATEO: [*offstage*] What?

CARINA: Get out here!

MATEO. [*offstage*] I'm on the phone!

CARINA: Get out here now!

BREYTHE: Bunna!!!

      MATEO *enters.*

MATEO: What? I'm on the phone to Mr Yukovich. What's going on? Where have you been?

BREYTHE: One-eight-one Hay street! Nglay!

MATEO: Hey!

BREYTHE: It's a joke not a dick, don't take it so hard.

MATEO: Oi! … Can I call you back? … Thank you … Where's he been?

CARINA: Guddayulla rocked up like this, he's off his face.

BREYTHE: Been living like a fringy! Made a ninni humpy on Nanny Goat Hill!

CARINA: Sort this out.

MATEO: Oi come here. Get inside … Come here.

BREYTHE: Don't touch me. I'm fine. I'm fine. Gone back to the land. Nomad. No. Mad!

MATEO: Breythe—

BREYTHE: What goorta? That's what you want isn't it? Get back to country …

CARINA: Mateo get him out of here. I don't want Mum to see him like this … Mateo!

BREYTHE: What's wrong?

CARINA: You're drunk!

BREYTHE: I'm soberer than a priest on Sunday … Don't I look all right? …

MATEO: Need to go and have a sleep.

BREYTHE: Did you see my big solid ad?

CARINA: Yeah …

BREYTHE: You like it? Showing my Aussie Aussie spirit. Huh? … Woo! Your silence is deafening. Think I heard a pin drop.

CARINA: It … was good—

BREYTHE: Liar.

CARINA: No—

BREYTHE: Talk shit! It was some coonary-bafoonary and you know it.

MATEO: Don't worry about what people say.

BREYTHE: Why? What are people saying?

MATEO: Nothing—

BREYTHE: I know what they're saying. I got Facebook you know! Twitter! Instagram! Snapchat! TikTok!

BREYTHE *flosses.*

CARINA: Don't worry about them—

MATEO: Yeah! Fuck em!

CARINA: They don't know what you're going through.

BREYTHE: Sold-out. I'm a coconut.

CARINA: No you're not.

BREYTHE: Yes I am.

CARINA: No! You're not!

BREYTHE: I didn't even fight them. Just did it.

CARINA: Hey! You know who you are. You're my little brother. You're a Wongi—

MATEO: Yeah! How many of those cunts can say they know their land, their language, their culture? We'll go bush right now. Shoot a marlu. And you'll skin it and cook it. How many of those keyboard warrior, urban blackfulla bitches can do that?

CARINA: You did it because you had to. For your family. For Dad …

Beat.

We're burying him tomorrow. We have a funeral, paid for, because of you. Dad forgave you … Now snap out of it! People said some shit about you, whatever! Suck it up! People been running our family down our whole lives … You did it. Now forget it ….

CARINA *looks at* MATEO. MATEO *doesn't know how to respond.*

MATEO: Stronger than me, man …

BREYTHE: I don't want to be here anymore.

MATEO: Come on, don't talk like that—

BREYTHE: What? No—

CARINA: Breythe—

BREYTHE: No! I don't want to be in town. Want to go bush … Want to feel the breeze on my face. Smell the salt in the air … I can't breathe … Sorry. I'm talkin' shit …

Beat.

CARINA: Why don't you two go for a ride? Out to Gidji or something? I'll sort out this stuff for tomorrow …

MATEO: You sure?

CARINA: Go on … Where's your stuff? Where's your bag?

BREYTHE: McCleery Street.

CARINA: That old house?

BREYTHE: Yeah … Wanted to sleep in old my room.

CARINA: Okay. You weirdo … Righto.

CARINA *pushes* BREYTHE *towards the car.*

See ya later …

BREYTHE *exits.*

Mateo! You two need to be here first thing tomorrow morning. Don't fuck around.

MATEO *leaves.* CARINA *watches on then walks to the door. Stops. A willie wagtail is twittering.* CARINA *stares at the bird for a while. Watches its every move.*

What do you want mamu? Shoo! Get lost. Don't come around here …

CARINA *looks back. Heads inside. Lightning lights up the sky. Rain starts to fall. A storm.*

SCENE FIVE

Funeral. 'Have you ever seen the rain' by Creedence Clearwater Revival plays, as CARINA, MATEO, CLIFFHANGER *and* BREYTHE *stand in a line. One by one they drop rose petals into the open grave. The men then take shovels, start to bury dirt on top.*

SCENE SIX

Funeral night. Mum's house. BREYTHE *and* CARINA *are seated in chairs, while* MATEO *is on a stool near the dartboard, betting on a sports-bet app.*

CARINA: I am absolutely drained.

BREYTHE: Over three hundred people there today. I'm sore from all the hugs and handshakes. Why blackfullas got the biggest families, ay? That many kids kept comin' up saying 'Hello Uncle Breythe'. I was like 'whose kid's this?' You can tell by their face, whose family, but I was like, 'Oh hello bub'.

CARINA: You were on *Home and Away*.

BREYTHE: Don't know why blackfullas watch that crap.

CARINA: Ask Mateo.

MATEO: Watch it with the missus … sometimes.

BREYTHE: Shame.

MATEO: Nigga you was on the show!

BREYTHE: Usually when you go funeral, you're comforting the family. Different experience on the other side.

CARINA: I was comforting other people. Halfway through I stopped crying.

BREYTHE: See the Spring mob? Wongi crying. Throwing themselves on the ground.

CARINA: Yeah, saw Aunty Wendy hitting herself in the head with that yabu. She going to have the biggest headache …

MATEO: You not s'posed to look. Forcin' it for respect.

BREYTHE: Freaks me out every time.

MATEO: Lotta people who weren't there. Won't forget that.

BREYTHE: Where was Aunty Pattie, nadoo?

CARINA: Sick. Diabetes.

MATEO: No excuse, you have to make it to funerals.

CARINA: She's only got one leg.

BREYTHE: Nadoo.

CARINA: Her kids could have given her a lift. Some people got no respect for old people …

BREYTHE: Fair few of Dad's work mates were there.

CARINA: Yeah, one of them came up with photos.

BREYTHE: Where? …

> CARINA *hands* BREYTHE *the photos.*

That's a good one …

CARINA: Pass it here. I'll put them away. Look at them later.

BREYTHE: Everyone at the cuppa tea, kept saying 'your dad was such a lovely man …'

CARINA: I've heard it all!

MATEO: Ay!

CARINA: Dad was the world's biggest whinger.

MATEO: No he wasn't.

CARINA: Was so. Just because someone dies doesn't make them a saint. Only last minute became sentimental. First time he text 'I love you', he freaked us out.

BREYTHE: It was a bit weird, ay? Nice in the end, though.

CARINA: Not complaining.

MATEO: Stop running him down then.

CARINA: Having a yarn, jeez.

BREYTHE: Yeah we're being gammon.

CARINA: Gammon? Listen to you, ya big Koori—

BREYTHE: I can't help it. I say gammon and deadly now. Too far gone. It's funny ay, you notice all the small differences, state to state. Here you say 'drink fountain'. Over there, they say 'bubbler'.

MATEO: What the hell is 'bubbler'?

BREYTHE: You know at school.

CARINA: They don't make bubbles—

BREYTHE: I know!

CARINA: That's stupid.

BREYTHE: Ay? And instead of 'polony', they have 'devon'.

MATEO: Devon? What's devon?

BREYTHE: It's like polony. Processed meat.

MATEO: Devon? That sounds a bit too flash.

BREYTHE: That's what I said to them blackfullas over there. And they were giving me shit, saying polony sounds flash.

MATEO: Polony?

BREYTHE: Yeah like it sounds Italian or something. 'Pol-lo-ni'.

CARINA: Racist.

MATEO: Make me wanna have a polony sandwich now.

BREYTHE: Yeah, ay? Coat it in tomato sauce. With cordial, there on the side …

CARINA: Not good for you.

MATEO: It's not there because it's good for ya. You eating it because you broke.

BREYTHE: Same time it's lovely when ya starvin' for a feed. When you broke, the simplest feed is lovely, ay?

MATEO: Grew up livin' on cereal.

BREYTHE: I remember when we were kids, it being off pay week and asking Mum 'what's for dinner?' 'Same thing you had yesterday …'

ALL: 'Toast!'

BREYTHE: Any time my white friends would come over, they'd ask, 'Hey Breythe, what's for lunch?' And I'd be like 'Why what? You hungry? Have a look in the cupboard, Weet-Bix there.'

All laugh.

MATEO: Hungry now.

CARINA: Didn't you two have a feed at the cuppa tea?

BREYTHE: I got caught up with that Noel fulla. Yarn your head off …

The all groan.

Dad worked with a lot of whitefullas, not sure he liked a lot of white people though.

Beat.

CARINA: Bloke was mad as a cut snake …

MATEO: Wasn't 'The Wild Man from Borneo' for nothing.

BREYTHE: Why did they call him that?

MATEO: Because on the footy field, he'd run straight through ya.

CARINA: Plus, he looked like a hippy.

BREYTHE: How does that make him from Borneo?

CARINA: Orangutans are from Borneo.

BREYTHE: Eh, big Planet of the Apes …

CARINA: You two now, Bangers and Mash.

BREYTHE/MATEO: [*singing*] 'Bangers and Mash, Bangers and Mash, them chimps are imps there aint no doubt. Bangers and Mash.'

CARINA *can't take their singing and leaves.*

BREYTHE: Should've played Acca-Dacca today, as we lowered Dad's body to 'I'm on the Highway to hell'. Just for all them churchies.

MATEO: Haha. I'm gonna play Charlie Pride at yours. There now black country singer!

BREYTHE: Err! At yours I'll play 'Another One Bites the Dust' …

MATEO: Haha. Na. At yours I'm gonna play 'Ding Dong the Witch is Dead' …

BREYTHE: Haha … Have you ever been to a whitefulla's funeral?

MATEO: Whitefullas don't die.

BREYTHE: Yeah. They get cremated.

MATEO: Wandi. I want my body to be buried. Return my spirit to the earth.

BREYTHE: You believe in spirits eh?

MATEO: Yeah.

BREYTHE: Bunna Mumu there!

MATEO *recoils.*

MATEO: Ay, what's wrong with you? You want to get grabbed?

BREYTHE: Wongis invented mumus to get kids to go to bed. 'Shut up now! Or that mumu gonna grab you!' Traumatise you to sleep.

MATEO: You'll believe it when you see it …

BREYTHE: What's willie wagtail then?

MATEO: Messenger bird! Telling you, you somewhere you shouldn't be. Something bad gonna happen. Someone's sick, someone's died …

BREYTHE: I saw a willie wagtail the day Dad died … Looked straight at me.

MATEO: You getting all the signs …

> *Beat.*

BREYTHE: Have you ever thought, I might look up to you?
MATEO: I'm gonna head off …

> MATEO *stands. Then so does* BREYTHE.

BREYTHE: You going to the drinks at the Cricketer's Club?
MATEO: After. Might go home and have quick nap first.
BREYTHE: Catch up with the missus?
MATEO: Had too much to drink for that. It'll be like playing pool with a rope.
BREYTHE: Not what I meant. And too much information.
MATEO: I wanna have a lay down. Meet you mob over there, ay? Cliffhanger's on his way.
BREYTHE: Righto …
MATEO: His birthday tomorrow. How long you in town for?
BREYTHE: I dunno. I want to stay. But, gotta get back to the grind, so soon.
MATEO: If you serious, about lore …
BREYTHE: Yuwa …

> *They shake hands and* MATEO *exits.*

SCENE SEVEN

Black Station. Headlights of a car. A masked MATEO *with a knife in his back pocket, drags in a tied and gagged* ANDREWS *with a bag on his head.* ANDREWS' *shouts are muffled.*

MATEO *ties* ANDREWS *to a chair and removes the bag from his bloodied face and strips the tape from his mouth.*

ANDREWS: Aah! What the fuck! … Shit. My fucken head … Where am I! What the fuck?

> ANDREWS *struggles in the chair.*

What the fuck? Where am I? Where the fuck am I? … People are going to be looking for me, you know. You're going to be in a lot trouble … If you let me go now. I'll forget all about this.

Forget anything happened.

MATEO *starts to take the mask off.* ANDREWS *is forcing his eyes closed.*

Don't do that!

MATEO: Open your eyes.

ANDREWS: No.

MATEO: Open your eyes.

ANDREWS: No …

MATEO: Look at my face …

ANDREWS: No! … Then you won't let me go! …

MATEO *forces* ANDREWS *to look at him but* ANDREWS *tries to resist.*

MATEO: Andrews, look at my face!!!

MATEO *has* ANDREWS' *attention.*

Do you know who I am?

ANDREWS: No …

MATEO: Have a good look …

ANDREWS: I don't know.

MATEO: Do you think I look like him?

ANDREWS: I don't know who you're talking about.

MATEO: Yes you do! … You know exactly who I'm talking about … He was a good man! My gurta! The men in my family, are good men. But I'm not.

ANDREWS: Yes you are. Yes you are. You are!

MATEO: No I'm not. Look at where you are. I'm a twisted horrible black cunt!

ANDREWS: Help! Help! Help!

MATEO *starts laughing.*

MATEO: Do you know what Gina Gudbi means? Oi! … Gina Gudbi?!

ANDREWS *shakes his head.*

ANDREWS: No …

MATEO: Say it … Go on. For fun … Gina Gudbi … Say it!

ANDREWS: Jidda Gutbee.

MATEO: Didn't hear you.

ANDREWS: Jeena Gudbi.

MATEO: No Gina … Gudbi …

ANDREWS: Gidda Gudbi.

MATEO: No watch my mouth. Gin-na … Gud-bi.

ANDREWS: Gina Gudbi.

MATEO: Yuwo! Gina Gudbi. Means feather foot! Gina Gudbi use feathers on their feet to cover their tracks. And guess what, cunt? You're in the middle of nowhere …

ANDREWS: It was an accident … I didn't mean to. I didn't mean to … I was scared.

MATEO: Scared?!

ANDREWS: I'm sorry. I'm so sorry!

MATEO: Sorry won't bring him back—

ANDREWS: I know! It was a mistake. A stupid mistake …

MATEO: Shut your fucking mouth! You were going to live your life like nothing ever happened—

ANDREWS: No. No. No. Please. Please don't. Please don't do this. No.

MATEO: This what happens when you push and push and push.

> CARINA *calls out.*

CARINA: Mateo!!!

> MATEO *is caught off guard.*

Mateo!

MATEO: Don't come in here Carina!

ANDREWS: Help!

> MATEO *hits* ANDREWS.

MATEO: Shut the fuck up!

ANDREWS: Mmm …

> CARINA *enters.*

CARINA: Mateo.

MATEO: Get out of here Carina …

CARINA: Mateo, what the fuck are doing!

MATEO: Get out of here Carina! …

CARINA: Mateo—

MATEO: He killed him Carina. He killed him!!!

CARINA: I know. I know. Goorta, I know. But you have to let him go.

MATEO: He has to pay for what he's done! He has to pay. It's my responsibility!

CARINA: No it's not. No … I know you think it is …. But it's not … This is their mess … You're right, Mateo. Nothing is ever going to change. It never will … But you have to let him go. You kill him, you not punishing him … You punishing your dithi. Your gurri. Your ngunthu … And me … Please let him go …

   Beat.

MATEO: Carina, I can't let him go …

   Beat.

CARINA: Then Mateo, I let you go …

   CARINA *leaves. Beat.*

MATEO: Carina … Carina!

   Long beat. MATEO *lets* ANDREWS *free.* ANDREWS *runs.* MATEO *is on his own. A single flicker of red and blue light glide across* MATEO's *face.*

SCENE EIGHT

BREYTHE *and* CLIFFHANGER *are on the street, outside the club.* BREYTHE *is on the phone.*

BREYTHE: Oi, we're outside … Me and Cliffhanger … Na, they wouldn't let us in … Same old, same old … What—

   CLIFFHANGER *staunch.*

CLIFFHANGER: Whatchyu lookin at you dum cun—

BREYTHE: Oi shut the fuck up! Don't do that! … We're gonna cruise home … Yeah we're gonna head up to the taxi rank now … Na Cliffhanger needs to go home. He's pissed.. What, you coming out now? Righto then … Yeah …

   BREYTHE *puts the phone down.*

What are you doing dumb cunt?

CLIFFHANGER: You dum cun. I'm not dum cun. Fucken—

   CLIFFHANGER *whistles.*

BREYTHE: Eh what are you doin' silly bastard? Whistling up womans, pickin fights …

CLIFFHANGER: I wanna moin.

BREYTHE: Well you not gonna get one actin' like that.

CLIFFHANGER: Fuck you. I'll fight you drunk prick.

BREYTHE: Err chippin'. Look at ya, can't even stand up …

CLIFFHANGER *shapes up.* Then so does BREYTHE.

Wouldn't be able to hit me anyway.

BREYTHE *and* CLIFFHANGER *spar.*

Too fast for ya, too pretty. I'm Ali brother. I'm Ali.

BREYTHE *'s dodging* CLIFFHANGER *'s jabs.*

CLIFFHANGER: Fuck you drunk prick. I'm Bruise Lee, I'm Bruise Lee … Oh you got skinny leg jeans. Can't move. Too tight, too tight.

BREYTHE: Yeah like that shirt around your guts.

CLIFFHANGER: Err fuck you …

BREYTHE *and* CLIFFHANGER *playfully tussle.*

BREYTHE: Finish now, finish now.

CLIFFHANGER *hooks his arm around* BREYTHE *'s neck.*

CLIFFHANGER: I lub you cunt … Miss you.

BREYTHE: Yeah I miss you too.

CLIFFHANGER: Miss my uncle rest in peace to God.

BREYTHE: Yeah, yeah I miss him too.

CLIFFHANGER: Proud of you. Proud of you.

BREYTHE: Yeah—

CLIFFHANGER: Listen—

BREYTHE: Yeah I am—

CLIFFHANGER: No listen, fuck you. Proud of you. You get out, this shithole.

BREYTHE: Yeah thank you.

CLIFFHANGER: Lub you my bruva, lub you.

BREYTHE: Yeah. I love you too. Bunna!

CLIFFHANGER: No fuck you. I lub you. No-one listen to me.

BREYTHE: I'm listening to you—

CLIFFHANGER: No! No-one listen to me. Everyone think I'm dum cun. All der time—

BREYTHE: I'm listening. I listening to you—

CLIFFHANGER: Yeah but you gone, don't live here anymore.

BREYTHE: I know.

CLIFFHANGER: Your dad look after me, and you, and you brother and you sister, and you mum.

BREYTHE: Yeah I know.

CLIFFHANGER: Everyone pick on me.

BREYTHE: Don't worry 'bout them. Do your own thing. Fuck them.

CLIFFHANGER: Yeah. And fuck you.

BREYTHE: Fuck you too.

CLIFFHANGER: You come my birffday tomorrow. Okay?

BREYTHE: Yeah.

CLIFFHANGER: Good.

BREYTHE *and* CLIFFHANGER *embrace.*

Err you gay try to hug me. And you skinny leg jeans.

BREYTHE: Shut the fuck up.

CLIFFHANGER *slumps to the curb.*

Yeah good, sit down now … But don't go sleep. I'm not carrying you.

CARINA *enters.*

CARINA: What happened now? Wouldn't let you in?

BREYTHE: Na Cliffhanger's too drunk …

CARINA: You wouldn't have got in with those shoes anyway.

BREYTHE: What's wrong my shoes?

CARINA: You know how they go.

BREYTHE: Probably a good thing we didn't get in. Uncle was sittin' here telling me he loves me.

CARINA: Oh nadoo …

BREYTHE: Misses me and Dad and how he loves us all.

CARINA: Winyarn …

BREYTHE: People still pick on him?

CARINA: Course they do. If you're not like everyone else, you're the butt of the jokes …

CARINA *waves Bye!*

BREYTHE: Who's that?

CARINA: Natalie? My old friend from school. She was at the funeral today ... Err. Don't be gross.

BREYTHE: What?

CARINA: What's wrong with you?! She's my friend.

BREYTHE: Wasn't even doing anything—

CARINA: She's an old woman; like me. Go for people your own age ... And don't go for white girls.

BREYTHE: What?

CARINA: Get a black woman.

BREYTHE: It's hard when I'm related to every black woman in the state!

CARINA: Get a Koori woman or something. Don't get a white woman.

BREYTHE: Listen to you ... You big racist.

CARINA: I can't be racist.

BREYTHE: Oh yes you can. Black people can be racist.

CARINA: I never said black people can't be racist. I said I can't be.

BREYTHE: What?!

CARINA: Anyway, what are we doing?

BREYTHE: Well we'll grab a cab, eh?

CARINA: Us three? Get a taxi? Dream on Niggariginal! Taxis aren't going to stop for us.

BREYTHE: Get your friend to do it.

CARINA: What?

BREYTHE: Get your friend to get the taxi.

CARINA: You just want her to come over here, so you can try to get her to go home with you.

BREYTHE: No! We'll wait over here and she can hail it down. Then when the taxi stops, we'll run up and jump in the back. Use her whiteness.

CARINA: Who's the racist now?

BREYTHE: I told you black people are racist.

CARINA: No. Shame ... I'm gonna go to Monty's and get a kebab.

BREYTHE: Err you grub ...Well how we gonna get home?

CARINA: Ask Mum to pick us up.

BREYTHE: No she might be in bed.

CARINA: You know she'll pick up 'Prince Breythe'.
BREYTHE: Oh fuck off.
CARINA: Ring her and I'll go get a feed.
BREYTHE: Well hurry up then. I'll call her now.
CARINA: You want anything?
BREYTHE: Um … just get me whatever you're gettin'.
CARINA: And what's balu doing?
BREYTHE: Get him the same.

> CARINA *puts her hand out.*

And what I'm paying for it?
CARINA: Derr …
BREYTHE: No shame.
CARINA: Breythe. Dad's gone now. Who do you think I'll be hitting up from now on? You're my retirement plan …

> BREYTHE *pulls out his wallet and takes out a note.* CARINA *grabs the cash out of the wallet instead.* BREYTHE *stands in disbelief.* CARINA *snatches the note in his hand too.*

BREYTHE: I'll find you a nice home!
CARINA: Thank you.

> CARINA *exits.*

> BREYTHE *puts his wallet back into his pocket as he turns to* CLIFFHANGER.

BREYTHE: Oi! Don't go sleep … Cliffhanger. Wake up. Cliffhanger!
CLIFFHANGER: Oi!
BREYTHE: Good. Don't go to sleep now. Stay awake.

> CLIFFHANGER *groans.*

Carina is going to get us a feed.

> CLIFFHANGER *gets up. Staggers.*

You right?
CLIFFHANGER: I got to piss.
BREYTHE: What?

> CLIFFHANGER *groans as he starts to urinate against the wall.*

Eh, Bunna! What you doin', don't go— Oh! Goonda! Shame we

out in public, fuck ya! … Oh shit … Well hurry up then before we get seen.

CLIFFHANGER *groans and sighs in relief.*

Shame …

BREYTHE *spots the police.*

Bunna! Hurry up. Boodi there. Cliffhanger hurry the fuck up, the cops are here …

CLIFFHANGER *can't hear* BREYTHE.

Oh shit. Cliffhanger. Shit.

The police arrive and walk up to the boys.

SIMMONDS: How are you gentlemen this evening?
BREYTHE: Yeah, good we're just—
SIMMONDS: Oi you. What are you doin'?
BREYTHE: Oh look sir, he's just taking a … leak.
SIMMONDS: Oi you!
BREYTHE: Yeah look, he's actually—
ANDREWS: He's not talking to you!
BREYTHE: Sorry …
SIMMONDS: Oi you against the wall, turn around.
BREYTHE: Yeah look he can't hear you, he's deaf.
ANDREWS: Are you deaf?
BREYTHE: No, he's deaf—
ANDREWS: Are you being a smart arse?
BREYTHE: No, he's actually deaf—
ANDREWS: Stand up against the wall.
BREYTHE: What? Why?
ANDREWS: Do it!

BREYTHE *backs up.*

SIMMONDS: What are you doing?
BREYTHE: Oi Cliffhanger.
SIMMONDS: Quiet. Turn around.

SIMMONDS *approaches* CLIFFHANGER. *Attempts to turns him around.*

CLIFFHANGER: Ah! Bruce Lee!

CLIFFHANGER *spins and mistakenly playfully chops* SIMMONDS' *chest like Bruce Lee.*

SIMMONDS *hits* CLIFFHANGER *in the stomach and* CLIFFHANGER *buckles to the ground.*

BREYTHE: No! No!

SIMMONDS: Stop resisting.

BREYTHE *goes to move.*

BREYTHE: No!

ANDREWS: Stay there and shut up.

SIMMONDS: Stop resisting.

BREYTHE: He can't hear you he's deaf—

SIMMONDS *starts to pat* CLIFFHANGER *down.*

SIMMONDS: Shut the fuck up! Are you concealing any weapons? Any dangerous items, any drugs or alcohol on your person?

ANDREWS: Stay there, he's got everything under control—

SIMMONDS *kicks* CLIFFHANGER.

BREYTHE: Whoa he just fucking kicked him! That's excessive!

ANDREWS: Stand back.

BREYTHE: Or what? You gonna mace me? /

SIMMONDS: Stay still!

BREYTHE: What's your names? I want to know your names, right now!

ANDREWS: That's Sergeant Simmonds and I'm Constable Andrews.

BREYTHE: Well Constable Andrews, I'm sober, he's drunk and we were seriously about to leave—

CLIFFHANGER: Aah! Get off you cunts!

BREYTHE: Hey come on! Fuck sake!

ANDREWS: I can arrest you for that.

BREYTHE: For what? For telling you to get fucked? Get fucked!

CLIFFHANGER *is murmuring on the ground as* SIMMONDS *tries to apprehend him.*

SIMMONDS: Get him on the ground! Move it boy. Get on the ground! Get him on the ground!

ANDREWS *forcefully takes* BREYTHE *down to the ground.* BREYTHE *complies.*

BREYTHE: You've got to be kidding me … Cliffhanger look at me.

ANDREWS *cuffs* BREYTHE *as* CLIFFHANGER *and* SIMMONDS *struggle.*

SIMMONDS: Stop resisting! Stop resisting! Stop resisting!

BREYTHE: Just calm down for fuck sake.

SIMMONDS *presses* CLIFFHANGER's *face into the ground.*

CLIFFHANGER: Aaaah!!!

CARINA *enters.*

CARINA: Hey what's going on?! What's going on?!

ANDREWS *is holding* BREYTHE's *hands behind his back and pinning him with a knee.*

ANDREWS: Stay back please. Stay back please. / Stay back now.

BREYTHE: Cliffhanger was takin' a piss and now they're losing their shit!

SIMMONDS: You need to stand back, / you need to stand back now.

CARINA: Can you tell me why you're on them? Why you're all over them? / What is going on?

ANDREWS: You need to stand back! You need to stand back now!

SIMMONDS *is putting more weight and pressure onto* CLIFFHANGER's *back.*

CLIFFHANGER: Oh fuck you cunt! I can't breathe, you fuck! I can't breathe!

SIMMONDS: If you can talk, you can breathe!

BREYTHE: He can't breathe, you fucken arsehole! / He can't breathe!

CARINA: You need to get off him.

CLIFFHANGER: Aah!

CARINA: He's got a condition! Listen to me! / He's got a condition!

CARINA *moves forward.*

BREYTHE: Oh get off him, you fucken cunts!

CARINA: Breythe shut up! Shut up! Can you get off him? He can't breathe! / He can't breathe.

SIMMONDS: Stand back, stand back! Get her back! Get her away!

ANDREWS *pulls out his handcuffs and locks* BREYTHE's *hands.*

ANDREWS *moves to* CARINA. CARINA *pulls out her phone and starts to record.*

CARINA: Don't touch me! I'm recording! I'm recording! I'm filming the whole thing!

SIMMONDS: Stop resisting!

CLIFFHANGER: I can't breathe! Can't breathe.

CARINA: He can't breathe! He's got a condition!

BREYTHE: / Carina—

CARINA: He's gonna have a fit! Holy shit, can you please get off him?

BREYTHE: / Carina—

CLIFFHANGER: I. Can't … Breathe …

CARINA: Oh my god. Oh my god!

CLIFFHANGER *is flopping and convulsing as* SIMMONDS *and* ANDREWS *try to apprehend him.* BREYTHE *makes his way up to stand and is still.* BREYTHE *rushes* SIMMONDS.

BREYTHE: Aah!

BREYTHE *kicks* SIMMONDS *off* CLIFFHANGER. ANDREWS *pulls out his gun. BANG!*

ANDREWS *shoots* BREYTHE. CARINA *screams.*

ANDREWS: Oh shit.

BREYTHE *slumps to the ground.* CARINA *runs to* BREYTHE.

BREYTHE : Carina … It's alright. It's alright. Stay the course …

Blackout.

THE END

www.ingramcontent.com/pod-product-compliance
Lightning Source LLC
Chambersburg PA
CBHW050021090426

42734CB00021B/3358